In partnership with

CW00656446

11+
Success
for
CEM

Results Booster

Targeted Practice Book

Philip McMahon

Contents

Guidance for Parents

The CEM (Durham University) 11+ Exam

CEM (The Centre for Evaluation and Monitoring) is part of Durham University. It is one of the two major bodies responsible for setting 11+ tests. Their tests are being used by an increasing number of selective schools in England.

The CEM exam consists of two papers and in each paper pupils are tested on their skills in verbal, non-verbal and numerical reasoning. Exams are separated into small, timed sections delivered by audio instructions.

It appears the content required for CEM exams changes from year to year, and the level at which pupils are tested ranges from county to county. Before sitting the exam, your child should be well prepared, with solid foundations built in the three core skills.

11 Plus Tutoring Academy

This book has been produced in partnership with 11 Plus Tutoring Academy.

11 Plus Tutoring Academy offers tuition and mock exams specifically for the Durham CEM 11+ exam in Gloucestershire, Buckinghamshire and other areas in the UK and overseas. They are one of the leading providers of tuition and mock exams for Durham CEM 11+ exams in the UK.

The Results Booster Book

The book focuses on the core skills needed for the CEM exam: verbal, non-verbal and numerical reasoning. It is divided into short, timed tests with CEM-style questions. The focus is on improving your child's awareness of working under timed conditions and includes time-management tips.

How and when to use the book

This book provides focused practice at the stage before your child sits mock tests either at home or with a specialist provider. We also publish practice test papers for the CEM 11+ exams, which include audio instructions that replicate the experience of the exam.
Visit www.collins.co.uk/letts11plus for the full range.

We suggest that your child writes the answers on a separate piece of paper when attempting this test for the first time, as you may want your child to complete this test again at a later date.

You should record your child's first attempt at each test in the table at the end of the book. At a later date, your child should repeat any section where the score was poor or if they were unable to finish.

The time allowed for each section is set to be challenging, but eventually manageable for your child. Depending on the amount of practice of timed tests which your child has completed prior to using this book, initially your child may find the tests difficult to complete. However, it is through practice of timed tests that pupils gain more confidence and become more time-aware. Writing answers on a separate piece of paper allows the tests to be re-used.

What your child will need:

A quiet place to do the tests
A clock/watch which is visible to your child
A piece of paper (on which to write the answers)
A pencil
Your child should not use a calculator for any of these papers.

Numeracy & Problem Solving

Mixed Questions Test 1

NO CALCULATORS ALLOWED IN TESTS

TOP TIME MANAGEMENT TIPS

- Work out how long you have to answer each question.
- Try not to spend too much time on any one question.
- Be aware that some questions will take longer to work out than others. Try to keep to your time limits.

 ## INSTRUCTIONS

 You have 10 minutes to complete the following section.
You have 13 questions to complete within the time given.

EXAMPLE

What is 2 + 2?

The correct answer is 4.

(1) What is $\frac{1}{3}$ of 51? 17

(2) How many millilitres are there in 50 centilitres?

(3) On a compass, which bearing is directly opposite South-East?

(4) How many 18s can be taken away from 774? 48

(5) How long, in hours and minutes, is there between these two times?

09:45 and 18:25 (on the same day)   9h 20m

(6) What is the answer if I subtract $\frac{1}{2}$ of 39 from $\frac{1}{2}$ the number of days in August? 3

(7) It is going to be −4°C tonight and it was −7°C yesterday night. How much warmer is it tonight compared to last night? 3°C

8. If the perimeter of a square is 81 cm, what is its area? 4.5

9. What is the next triangular number after 21?

10. Calculate 142 x 24 2408

11. Calculate 65,260 divided by 13.

12. I save half of my weekly pocket money, give 10% to charity, and spend the rest. How much do I spend, if I give £1.20 to charity each week?

13. The roller blades I am saving up for have just been reduced in the sale by 15%. I had saved up half of the money I needed before they were reduced. If I have saved £60, how much more money do I need to save in order to buy the roller blades at the reduced sale price? £18

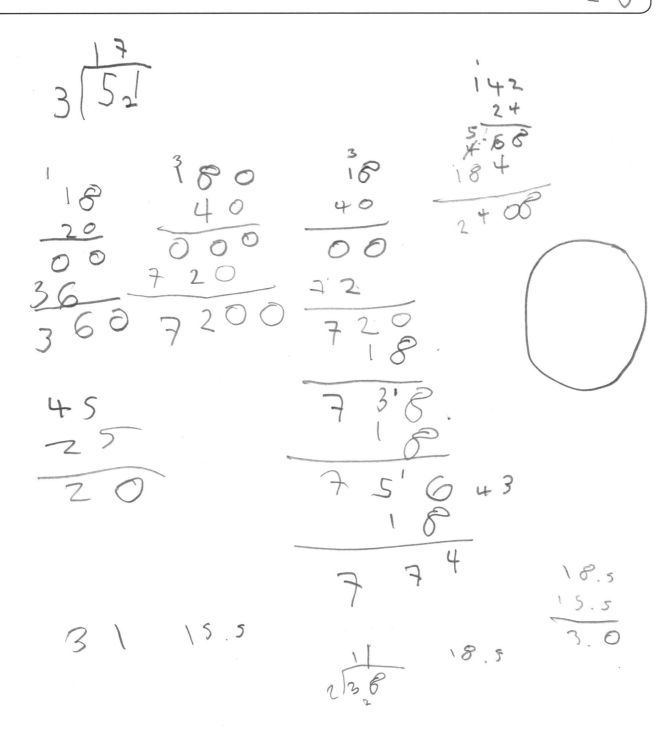

Mixed Questions Test 2

NO CALCULATORS ALLOWED IN TESTS

 INSTRUCTIONS

 You have 10 minutes to complete the following section.
You have 13 questions to complete within the time given.

(1) If $4x + 2y = 60$ and $2x + 2y = 36$

what is the value of y?

(2) Half the people at a party left before 8 pm and a further four people left before midnight. A third of the total guests remained.

How many people remained at the party after midnight?

(3) A supermarket sells different brands of tins of chopped tomatoes in different sizes and at various prices.

Look at the information and identify which size is the best value:

400 g at 60p
1200 g at £1.70
200 g at 32p
300 g at 42p
1 kg at £1.60

(4) A mother shares out some money between her three children in the following way:

The first child receives $\frac{1}{5}$ of the total.

The second child receives $\frac{1}{4}$ of the total.
The third child receives the remainder.

If the third child receives £132, what is the total amount of money that is shared out?

(5) The time in country A is 8 hours behind country B.

If country C is 4 hours ahead of Country A, what is the time difference between countries B and C?

(6) A cylindrical candle burns at a steady rate of 10 mm per hour.

The cross-sectional area of the candle is 2 cm².

If the candle takes 5 hours to burn completely from when it was first lit, what was the volume of the candle at the start?

(7) There are 29 children on a bus when it starts its journey.

17 children get off the bus at its first stop.
6 more get on at the first stop.
29 get on at the second stop
15 get off at the third stop
All of the children get off at the fourth stop.

How many children get off the bus at the fourth stop?

(8) Brian and Fiona's ages add up to 90 years.

If Brian is 8 years older than Fiona, how old are Brian and Fiona currently?

(9) 212 people visit a wildlife park between opening time and noon.

If there are 712 visitors during the entire day, how many people visit the park in the afternoon?

(10) A car has a fuel tank with a capacity of 15 gallons.

The tank is two-thirds full.
The car can travel 30 miles per gallon of fuel.

How many miles can the car travel before running out of fuel?

(11) What is the size of the obtuse angle between the hands of a clock showing 7 o'clock?

(12) On his next birthday, Tom will be 3 years younger than his older sister.

His older sister was 9 years old on Tom's last birthday.

How old will Tom be on his next birthday?

(13) Some of the digits in this subtraction have been replaced by *. Work out the value of the missing digits.

```
  6*4*
- *3*9
  ────
  4883
```

Mixed Questions Test 3

NO CALCULATORS ALLOWED IN TESTS

 INSTRUCTIONS

 You have 10 minutes to complete the following section.
You have 13 questions to complete within the time given.

① A mother shares out some money between her three children in the following way:

The first child receives 12.5% of the total.

The second child receives $\frac{3}{4}$ of the total.

The third child receives the remainder.

If the third child receives £190.50, how much did the first child receive?

② Terry is 5 years younger than Bernice.

Bernice will be twice as old as Georgie will be 1 year from now.
Terry was 71 last year.

How old is Georgie now?

③ There are 23 children on a bus when it starts its journey.

15 children get off the bus at its first stop.
9 more get on at the first stop.
6 get off at the second stop and more children get on.
All 18 remaining children get off at the third (and final) stop.

How many children got on the bus at the second stop?

④ A supermarket sells different brands of orange juice in different sizes and at various prices. Look at this information and identify which size is the best value.

1 litre at £1.35
500 millilitres at 90p
2 litres at £2.75
1.5 litres at £1.90
750 millilitres at £1.20

(5) A car has a fuel tank with a capacity of 90 litres.

The tank is 50% full.

If the car can travel 500 miles before running out of fuel, calculate the number of miles the car travels per gallon.
(Assume 1 gallon is equal to approximately 4.5 litres.)

(6) If an equilateral triangle has the same length side as a regular hexagon, how many of the equilateral triangles will fit inside the regular hexagon?

(7) 247 people visit a museum between 9 am (opening time) and noon, and 438 people visit between 3 pm and 7 pm (closing time).

If 927 people visit the museum in the entire day, how many visitors were there between noon and 3 pm?

(8) 70% of the people at a party leave by 3 pm and eight people leave just before 4 pm.

If the remaining people who leave after 4 pm make up one-tenth of the total guests, how many people leave the party after 4 pm?

(9) Which fraction is larger:

$\frac{5}{8}$ or $\frac{7}{12}$?

(10) If 3 pears and 3 apples cost £2.76 and 3 pears and 2 apples cost £2.26, what is the cost of 1 pear?

(11) The time in country A is 10 hours ahead of country B.

If country C is 4 hours behind Country A, what is the time difference between countries B and C?

(12) What is the size of the reflex angle between the hands of a clock showing the time 2 o'clock?

(13) Subtract the smallest of the following numbers from the largest number:

2.01   2.005   2.100   2.050   2.105

Problem Solving Test 1

NO CALCULATORS ALLOWED IN TESTS

TOP TIME MANAGEMENT TIPS

- Be aware that some of the answer options may be very similar so be careful when choosing an answer.
- Read the passage and the questions very carefully.

 INSTRUCTIONS

 You have 12 minutes to complete the following section.
You have 10 questions to complete within the time given.

Read the passage and then answer the questions that follow.
For each question, select the correct answer from the options given
in the table below. You may use an option more than once.

A £31,616	B 20	C 2 hours 18 minutes	D 66	E 43.2
F 1 hour 9 minutes	G 38	H 2 hours 22 minutes	I 189	J £148,800
K £30,400	L 42	M £158,080	N 156	O 264

Mira is a dentist. She studied dentistry at university from the end of September 2000 until the end of May 2006. She has been working in her current practice since the start of June 2006.

It is now the beginning of December 2011.

Mira's usual working hours are from 9 am until 6 pm Monday to Thursday (except one hour for lunch), and from 9 am until noon on Fridays and Saturdays. She does not work on Sundays. Mira is paid the equivalent of £80 per hour. Her dental assistant, Sandra, is paid one-fifth of what Mira is paid and works the same hours as Mira.

Sandra has to travel 1.5 hours door-to-door, from home to work (and back) each day she works. She travels by train and walks the final part of her journey. Her train to work departs at 07.42 and arrives at the station closest to her work at 08.51. The journey home is the same length in time. Sandra's train ticket, which is valid for the entire year, costs £9,450.

Sandra is considering driving to work. Her car travels 20 miles per gallon of petrol. The cost of petrol is £1 per litre and there are 4.5 litres in one gallon. The journey (each way) to work is 40 miles. The cost of parking is £26 each day, including weekends. The parking charge is always for the entire day and there is no reduction for parking for a shorter time.

1. For how many months has Mira been working in her current practice?

2. How many hours does Mira usually work in a week?

3. If Mira is paid for all weeks in the year, how much is Mira paid annually?

4. How much does Sandra get paid per year if she has two weeks of holiday which is unpaid?

5. What is Sandra's hourly rate as a percentage of Mira's hourly rate?

6. How long does Sandra spend on a train each day (assuming no delays)?

7. What is the weekly cost in pounds of train travel for Sandra when spread across the 50 weeks that she works?

8. What would the weekly parking cost in pounds be for Sandra for each of the 50 weeks she works?

9. What would Sandra's weekly travel costs be in pounds if she changed to travelling by car rather than by train? (The travel costs by car should include fuel and parking costs.)

10. If the cost of petrol increases by 40%, how much more would the weekly petrol cost be in pounds?

Problem Solving Test 2

NO CALCULATORS ALLOWED IN TESTS

 ## INSTRUCTIONS

 You have 12 minutes to complete the following section.
You have 10 questions to complete within the time given.

**Read the passage and then answer the questions that follow.
For each question, select the correct answer from the options given
in the table below. You may use an option more than once.**

A 2247	B 6	C 5	D 18	E 360
F 3500	G 567	H 120	I 26	J 3
K 1926	L 713	M 146	N 19	O 2

Stuart and Jenny are married. They married at the beginning of December 1997. It is now the end of November 2016.

Stuart is a barber and Jenny is a hairdresser. They each have separate businesses in different towns. Jenny's hairdresser's is in Slough and Stuart's barbershop is in Chesham. Stuart's barbershop is open from 8 am until 5 pm, Monday to Saturday.

Customers are charged £6 for a haircut in Stuart's shop. He is very busy, so he pays Juliet to help him with the haircuts. She is paid £7 per hour and works all the hours the shop is open, with the exception of a 1-hour break for lunch, which they both have each day.

Jenny's hairdresser's is open from 9 am until 6 pm from Monday to Sunday. Jenny pays two other hairdressers to help her (Jackie and Sally). They each work for £9 per hour and are paid for their lunch break. Jenny, Jackie and Sally work all the hours the hairdresser's is open. A haircut in Jenny's hairdresser's costs £20. There are no other services available.

Both hairdressers are open for 50 weeks each year. Each week, on average, there are the following number of customers:

- haircuts at Jenny's: 175 customers per week
- haircuts at Stuart's: 321 customers per week.

(1) How many years have Stuart and Jenny been married?

(2) Jackie started working at Jenny's hairdresser's 4 years ago exactly. Next year, Jackie will be half Jenny's age. Jenny is 45 this year and her birthday is the same day as Jackie's: 1 January.

How old was Jackie when she starting working at Jenny's hairdresser's?

(3) How much does Sally get paid in pounds each week?

(4) When there are no customers, Sally cuts Jenny's hair and Jenny cuts Sally's hair. If they do this for free every 2 months, how much do they each save in pounds on haircuts each year, compared to the price they charge the customers?

(5) Sally usually gets a £2 tip, on average, per customer. If she averages 73 haircuts per week, how much in pounds does she receive in tips each week?

(6) What is the total Sally receives from her pay and tips each week?

(7) One day, Jackie had a customer who was very upset because her hair had been cut too short. She complained to Jenny, who then agreed to give her a 30% discount off her next haircut, as well as not charging her for the haircut that day.

How much of a saving was this for the customer, assuming she did return to have her hair cut there in future?

(8) What is the total money received in pounds for haircuts at Jenny's on an average week?

(Assume no refunds.)

(9) What is the total money received in pounds for haircuts at Stuart's on an average week?

(Assume no refunds.)

(10) Stuart and Juliet take the same amount of time to complete each haircut. To the nearest whole number, on average, how many haircuts does Juliet complete per hour?

Problem Solving Test 3

NO CALCULATORS ALLOWED IN TESTS

 INSTRUCTIONS

 You have 12 minutes to complete the following section.
You have 15 questions to complete within the time given.

Read each problem and select one answer from the following answer options A–E.

(1) I need to arrive at the airport in New York by 8 pm and I am in London where the time is 5 hours ahead. The flight duration is 7 hours. Flights leave London hourly at 30 minutes past the hour.

Select the latest flight departure from the answer options below that I can get to arrive in New York by 8 pm at the latest, assuming no delays.

A	B	C	D	E
4.30 pm	6.30 pm	7.30 pm	5.30 pm	8.30 pm

(2) A bath is being filled. The water comes from the tap into the bath at a rate of 2 litres every 10 seconds.

How long will it take to fill a bath containing 70 litres of water?

A	B	C	D	E
5 minutes 50 seconds	3 minutes 50 seconds	35 seconds	35 minutes	3.5 minutes

(3) The petrol tank in my car shows I have 20 litres remaining at the start of my journey. The tank holds 80 litres when full.

What quantity of fuel remains after my journey, if my journey uses a quarter of a full tank of petrol?

A	B	C	D	E
$\frac{1}{4}$ litre	15 litres	5 litres	The tank is empty.	20 litres

(4) Calculate the following.

What is the greatest number of 9s that can be taken away from 404?

A	B	C	D	E
45	46	43	44	50

5

Destination	Train 1	Train 2	Train 3	Train 4
Carterton	08:09	09:51	11:31	17:03
Evenlode	08:34	10:25	–	–
Burford	09:14	11:19	12:42	18:11
Naunton	09:27	–	12:51	–
Daylesford	10:21	12:11	–	–
Stow	11:16	13:03	14:19	19:09

Which train is the slowest (in time) between Carterton and Stow?

A	B	C	D	E
Train 1	Train 3	Train 2	Train 5	Train 4

6 What is the probability of rolling one dice and scoring **more** than 3?

A	B	C	D	E
2 chances in 6	1 chance in 6	3 chances in 6	4 chances in 6	6 chances in 6

7 $a + 4b = 8$

Find b, if $a = 4$:

A	B	C	D	E
1	2	4	8	16

8 Find the expression for the nth term in the following sequence:

2, 3, 4, 5, 6...

A	B	C	D	E
$2n - 1$	$n - 1$	$2n$	7	$n + 1$

9 Look at the rectangle below, which shows the lengths of each side in centimetres.

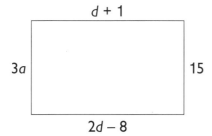

Calculate the area of the rectangle.

A	B	C	D	E
15 cm²	25 cm²	150 cm²	100 cm²	125 cm²

10 Solve the following equation to find the value of e:

$16 - e = 27$

A	B	C	D	E
11	−9	17	3	−11

(11) Solve the following equation to find the value of y:

$4y - 10 = 2$

A	B	C	D	E
−32	3	−2	42	36

(12) An unknown number n, is squared. The result has 17 added to it. The answer is 66. Find the value of n.

A	B	C	D	E
83	49	9	11	7

(13) Tom, Yasmin and Kerry played a game of dominoes. At the end of the game, Tom won two dominoes from Yasmin and Yasmin won three dominoes from Kerry.

At the start of the game, Tom had twice as many dominoes as Yasmin and Kerry had three times as many dominoes as Yasmin. There were 48 dominoes in total.

At the end of the game, how many dominoes did Kerry have?

A	B	C	D	E
22	21	9	18	27

(14) Sarah and her friend Kate took their children to the zoo. The total cost for the two adults and five children was £49.50. If the cost of a child ticket is half the cost of an adult ticket, find the cost of a child ticket.

A	B	C	D	E
£4	£5	£6	£6.50	£5.50

(15) Jeff has his 46th birthday today. How many months old is he?

A	B	C	D	E
552	460	506	550	542

Problem Solving Test 4

NO CALCULATORS ALLOWED IN TESTS

 INSTRUCTIONS

 **You have 10 minutes to complete the following section.
You have 10 questions to complete within the time given.**

Read the following passage, then answer the questions below.

Marjorie is redesigning her garden. Currently, her garden is all grass and is rectangular, measuring 24 m in length and 10 m in width. She would like to create a rectangular patio area in one corner measuring 5 m by 4 m.

At the other end of the garden, Marjorie is planning on having a small rectangular swimming pool with the dimensions 8 m by 4 m. The depth of the pool will be 1.5 m throughout.

There is also a small rectangular area where Marjorie would like to grow raspberries. This area measures 6 m by 1.5 m.

There will be a lavender border down both of the long sides of the garden. This will be 0.5 m wide on each side.

1. What is the total garden area? (You should include all areas of grass, borders, patio, fruit and the pool.)

2. What is the area of the pool?

3. What is the volume of the water in the pool when it is filled?

4. If each cubic metre of water weighs one tonne, how much does all the water in the pool weigh in tonnes?

5. What is the total area of the lavender borders?

6. To the nearest whole number, what percentage of the total garden area does the raspberry area amount to?

7. Using the fraction in its simplest terms, what is the denominator when working out the patio area as a fraction of the total garden area?

8. If the patio is made up of small square tiles that have a side measuring 10 cm, how many tiles would be required to cover the patio?

9. Tiles are sold in boxes of 70 and cost £65 per box. How much will it cost to pave the patio?

10. All areas of the garden that have not been changed remain as grass. What percentage (to the nearest whole number) of the total garden area is now grass after the changes?

Verbal Reasoning

Comprehension Test 1

TOP TIME MANAGEMENT TIPS

- As you are under time pressure, scanning through the questions first will help you to know what to look for in the passage.
- Don't forget that there may be some information in the text that is not relevant to any of the questions.
- Be aware of how much time you spend on any one question. If you think that you have already spent too much time on a question, guess – from sensible options – and move on to the next question.

 INSTRUCTIONS

 You have 15 minutes to complete the following section.
You have 10 questions to complete within the time given.

EXAMPLE

Anne bought some new slippers yesterday. They are red with pretty little bows at the front.

What colour are Anne's new slippers?
A   pink
B   blue
C   purple
D   red
E   brown

The correct answer is D.

Read the passage and then answer the questions that follow.

The Legacy of the 2012 Olympic Games

The year 2012 was an important one for Britain as it was the year that the Olympic Games were held in London.

Although the Games only lasted for 16 days, it took more than 7 years for London to prepare for them after it won the bid in 2005. It was a close-run bid between the cities of London, Madrid and Paris. Many felt that Moscow was also a contender.

The Olympic Torch Relay started in May and ended in July. It took 70 days for the torch to arrive at its final destination at the Olympic Stadium during the Opening Ceremony. In the lead-up to the Games, people watched the Olympic torch being paraded through their neighbourhood. Children were encouraged to take an interest in the Games by watching the Olympic torch visit their town.

Public opinion was divided when it came to the cost of the Olympic Games and, although many people were in favour of the Games, there was also some opposition to them. Many people were excited by the prospect of attending the Games, but this was offset by people who were sceptical about the long-term benefits of the Games. Some believed the huge cost of the Games was a financial burden and that only the people of London would benefit from them. The actual cost of the Games to every man, woman and child in the UK was just under £150. The final cost of the Games was just under £9 billion.

The Olympic Committee argued that there were a number of benefits to holding the Games in the UK. The first benefit directly affected the local area where the Olympic Games were being held, as the area near the Olympic Park would be regenerated. There can be no doubt that the local area of Stratford benefited greatly. What was once a deprived area with empty shops is now thriving with many new businesses. It was also stated that the UK as a whole would experience huge economic growth running into billions of pounds and that the effect would be felt for years to come.

Others commented on the direct impact it would have on the well-being of adults and children as there would be renewed interest in sport around the country.

A few years later, news stories continue to report on how the legacy of the Olympic Games is apparent, as many people have been inspired to try new sports. It was recently reported that rowing and cycling, which were previously perceived as being sports only for men, now have a huge female following. This is a direct result of the achievements of the British female Olympians.

Irrespective of people's personal thoughts on the financial impact that the Games would bring, there is no doubt that the Games brought communities together. It was the focus of the nation at all hours of the day and the television ratings were unprecedented. The Opening Ceremony ran for 3.5 hours and over 20 million people in the UK marvelled at this piece of British artistry, which included famous faces from television and film, as well as popular music and dramatic illuminations. Over 900 million people watched the ceremony worldwide.

The Games unified the nation as people watched new sports and experienced a feeling of patriotism towards the British athletes. It cannot be denied that it was a unique and memorable period which united people through sport. After the Games, gold post boxes were installed to mark the achievements of local athletes in their home towns and they are evocative reminders of that special summer. To celebrate the success of Team GB and Paralympics GB, the athletes attended a special event in London. Crowds lined the streets to watch floats containing the team members. The parade started in the City of London and ended outside Buckingham Palace.

Just under 11,000 athletes competed for almost 1000 medals and for many of these athletes, London 2012 represents the highlight of their career.

1 What is a similar word to 'contender'?

A   destroyer
B   arranger
C   challenger
D   surveyor
E   ranger

2 Which of these phrases best describes the journey of the Olympic torch?

A   It took over 2 months to arrive at the Opening Ceremony and it visited many places along the way.
B   It took less than 2 months to arrive at the Closing Ceremony.
C   It took over 4 months to arrive at the Opening Ceremony.
D   It took over 7 months to arrive at the Opening Ceremony.
E   It visited very few places before it arrived at the Closing Ceremony.

3 Which of these phrases best describes public opinion towards the London Olympic Games?

A   The public as a whole were pleased that the Olympic Games would be coming to our shores.
B   The public objected to the dates of the Olympic Games.
C   The government were unhappy about having to pay for the Olympic Games.
D   The public were happy to pay £150 towards the Olympic Games.
E   The public had mixed feelings about the overall cost of the Olympic Games.

4 What is the meaning of 'a person who is sceptical'?

A   A person who has reservations
B   A person who makes a reservation
C   A person who is reserved
D   A person who is convinced
E   A person who is certain

5 What has been the economic impact of the Olympic Games on the local area?

A   The local area has not received any economic benefit.
B   The local area is now rejuvenated.
C   The local area now has empty shops.
D   The local area is still deprived.
E   The passage does not say.

6 According to the news stories, what has been the impact of the London Olympic Games on sport?

    A   People do not watch new sports.

    B   People do not compete in any new sports.

    (C)   People now watch and follow a wider variety of sports.

    D   People only watch the sports in which they compete.

    E   The passage does not say.

7 What does the passage say about the Opening Ceremony?

    A   It was watched by a few people around the world.

    B   It was a mixture of history and places.

    C   It was a mixture of lights, music and people.

    D   It was a mixture of film and television.

    E   It was watched by very few people in the UK.

8 What type of word is 'evocative'?

    A   pronoun

    B   adjective

    C   noun

    D   verb

    E   adverb

9 How were the achievements of local athletes marked?

    A   The passage does not say.

    B   A special parade took place in London.

    C   A red post box was installed in London.

    D   A special post box was installed in the town in which they live.

    E   Street parties were held.

10 Which phrase best describes the meaning of the word 'unprecedented'?

    A   Without parallel

    B   Without preparation

    C   Without a dent

    D   Without a commentary

    E   Without a signal

Comprehension Test 2

INSTRUCTIONS

 You have 12 minutes to complete the following section.
You have 10 questions to complete within the time given.

Read the passage and then answer the questions that follow.

Jeremy's party

Jeremy had reached the ripe old age of 40 and his wife was secretly planning a party to celebrate this milestone in his life. Jeremy and Milly had been married for 14 years and had been at school together. Their paths didn't cross again for many years after they left school. It wasn't until they had both finished university that they met by chance, whilst playing tennis at their local club.

Despite being a witty man, Jeremy was reserved and disliked being the centre of attention. He was generally considered a mild-mannered, gentle fellow. Milly decided that she would hold Jeremy's 40th party at one of his favourite restaurants. It was a restaurant where they had been on many occasions before they were married.

The chosen venue was a country pub called 'The Cottage' in the middle of a tiny village near Windsor Castle. The pub was traditional in all senses of the word and epitomised the quaint English pub, serving traditional food. Jeremy and Milly had considered holding their wedding reception at this pub as it was an enchanting venue, but they soon realised that they would struggle to accommodate all of their 150 guests.

The day of Jeremy's birthday arrived and Milly followed the traditions set for his birthday. The day always started with a delicious birthday breakfast and a handcrafted birthday card, which Milly had decorated with quilling.

Jeremy then asked Milly what she had planned for his birthday. Milly apologised, pretending that she had not organised very much as she had been so busy with the children and her work. She had a lot of work as she had recently been given the honour of producing a set of cards for a national tourist attraction. Milly said that she had only managed to reserve a table at a new pizza restaurant. Jeremy felt disappointed by the supposed lack of thought, but he did not show this and politely thanked his wife for booking the table.

Two hours later, they set off for their quiet lunch. Milly did not realise that there would be so much traffic as she had not known about the country show which was being held in the grounds of the castle. There were many more vehicles on the road than she had anticipated and most of these were slow-moving vehicles such as horse boxes and tractors.

Milly had to contact the restaurant to inform them (and their guests) that they would be over an hour late. Jeremy was none the wiser and kept reassuring Milly that there would not be a problem as the restaurant would keep the table for them. Unbeknown to Jeremy, there were also thirty of his best friends from work, university and school waiting for him. Milly was feeling distressed and apprehensive. This was something she had not foreseen; she was a meticulous planner and had been preparing the party for the last 3 months.

Finally, Milly and Jeremy arrived at the restaurant over three hours late! By this time, Milly had been in tears for most of the journey, despite Jeremy's reassurances. By the time they arrived, Milly looked bleary-eyed and felt quite the opposite of elated, which was how she had hoped to feel.

As Jeremy opened the tiny door into the beamed restaurant, he stopped so as not to hit his head on the low ceiling. As he looked up, he saw the faces of all his friends smiling at him. At that moment, Milly was content and all her negative emotions floated away. Their friends hugged them both and Milly knew that the wonderful party she had planned could now begin. The afternoon was spent talking, laughing and reminiscing. Jeremy reached over to hold Milly's hand and whispered "Thank you for such a wonderful day".

1 What is the meaning of 'milestone' in the context of the passage?
- **A** A number of reference points
- **B** A significant event in a person's life
- **C** A roadside stone marking the distance from one place to another
- **D** An unimportant event in a person's life
- **E** A number of physical markers

2 Where did Jeremy and Milly meet again?
- **A** At the squash club
- **B** At university
- **C** At school
- **D** At college
- **E** At the tennis club

3 Which phrase best describes Jeremy's personality?
- **A** A quiet and amusing personality
- **B** A miserable and loud personality
- **C** A noisy and fun personality
- **D** A gentle but noisy personality
- **E** An extroverted personality

4 Where did Milly and Jeremy hold their wedding reception?
- **A** At Windsor Castle
- **B** The passage does not say
- **C** The Cottage
- **D** At an exquisite venue
- **E** At their home

(5) Which of these phrases best describes the usual way that Jeremy spends his birthdays?

 A With a delicious lunch

 B With a homemade breakfast only

 C With a delicious dinner

 D With a delicious lunch and a new handmade quilt

 E With a delicious breakfast and a handmade card

(6) What was Milly's recent project?

 A A set of handmade quilts for a national tourist attraction

 B A handmade quilt for a local tourist attraction

 C A handcrafted card for a local tourist attraction

 D A set of handcrafted cards for a national attraction

 E A set of handmade cards for a local attraction

(7) Why was there so much traffic on the road?

 A Due to tourists at the castle

 B Due to tractors moving from farm to farm

 C Due to a country show

 D Due to a broken-down horse box

 E Due to a party at the castle

(8) What is the meaning of the phrase 'none the wiser'?

 A To be calm about something

 B To be not calm about something

 C To be aware

 D To be clever

 E To be unaware

(9) How was Milly feeling when she arrived at the restaurant?

 A Upset and angry

 B Upset and nervous

 C Confident and positive

 D Bored and sad

 E Annoyed

(10) What type of word is 'unbeknown'?

 A adjective

 B adverb

 C noun

 D verb

 E pronoun

Comprehension Test 3

  INSTRUCTIONS

 **You have 12 minutes to complete the following section.
You have 10 questions to complete within the time given.**

Read the passage and then answer the questions that follow.

An interview with Hani

Here is an interview with Hani, who is 15 years old and takes an avid interest in the weather. Kathryn has interviewed Hani to find out his thoughts about the weather and how he hopes to be able to use his meteorological fascination in his chosen career.

Kathryn: Hani, can you tell me what particularly interests you about the weather?

Hani: I have always been fascinated by the weather, in particular, storms and their effect on nature and people.

Kathryn: Why are you particularly interested in storms?

Hani: When I was about 5 years old, I was on a holiday in the mountains of northern Italy. My parents and I were driving along the motorway when we saw a grey cloud overhead. The ominous cloud was located between two service stations. We stopped at the service station on our side of the motorway and, as soon as we stopped, the storm hit us. It sent hailstones the size of golf balls crashing down on our car, denting the bonnet and roof. From that day onwards, I have always been captivated by the power and intensity of a thunderstorm.

Kathryn: Have you ever experienced weather that frightened you?

Hani: On the same holiday in Italy, I had another electrifying experience during a thunderstorm. The holiday home in which we were staying was hit by a bolt of lightning one night. Luckily, the house had a lightning conductor. Normally, this would have caused a fire in the house. However, the lightning conductor did its job and we avoided a fire. As we were all awake, we opened the shutters and saw that there were forest fires blazing all around us. Lightning had obviously hit the trees and the forests were ablaze for about two days. We saw helicopters flying over us, collecting water from the sea and bringing it back to try and extinguish the fires. This was the most frightening experience, but it really made me notice the weather and how much of an impact it has on people's everyday lives.

Kathryn: Have you ever experienced any strange weather in your home town?

Hani: Yes. It occurred when I was out walking at the top of a hill that I can see from my house. As I stood in the car park, I saw a storm cloud moving quickly from the adjacent hill. I was so excited about the prospect of experiencing the eye of the storm that I asked my mum and dad if we could wait in the car park. I stood by my parents' car waiting for the storm. It didn't take long to reach us and I was amazed by the strength of the wind. It felt as though it could have blown me off the ground! As quickly as it had reached me, it had moved on and the weather was calm again. It was a really strange sensation, but I was not frightened at all. When we arrived home, we saw that our road had been completely flooded as a result of the storm. The drains were unable to clear the water from the road quickly enough and the water had reached our front step. If it had continued raining for any longer, the water would have come into our hall and into the lounge through a grille in the wall.

Kathryn: What is the most interesting fact you know about storms?

Hani: I once read that the heat in a bolt of lightning is hotter than the sun. Amazingly, people can survive when they are hit by lightning and some people have been hit more than once!

Kathryn: Are you going to be a meteorologist when you are older?

Hani: I used to dream of being a storm chaser in the USA, but my parents were worried that this would be very dangerous. I felt that it is not really a career, but more of a pastime. I also found out that in reality, despite their best endeavours, the storm chasers miss the storms. It also sounds rather tedious as it entails driving for many hours to find the storm and, more often than not, you miss it.

Kathryn: What is your career plan now?

Hani: As I do not want to limit my options, I would like to study Science at university. I can then decide whether to become a meteorologist or just keep weather as my hobby.

Kathryn: When do think you will next experience 'wild weather'?

Hani: The great thing about the weather is that you never know when the next storm will be! Sometimes you can have snow in April even though you think Spring has sprung. I recently read that you are more likely to have snow at Easter than Christmas. I like the unexpected and the weather always brings me something amazing. I am excited every day when I wake up!

Kathryn: Are you the only person who loves the weather in your family?

Hani: No, my mum and dad have always liked walking in the countryside as they like watching the change in seasons. It doesn't matter what the weather is like, they always go for a walk in all weathers. My little sister loves jumping in puddles and being out in the rain, so I suspect that she might like it too!

1 Which particular elements of the weather does Hani find most fascinating?
    A   Hani particularly likes rain and nature.
    B   Hani likes all elements of the weather.
    C   Hani likes hailstones and clouds.
    D   Hani particularly likes the strength of forest fires.
    E   Hani likes watching storms and how they affect nature.

2 What is the meaning of the word 'ominous'?
    A   calming
    B   threatening
    C   auspicious
    D   misaligned
    E   dangerous

3 When has Hani been most frightened by the weather?
    A   When he was at his neighbour's house and lightning struck
    B   When his friend was hit by lightning
    C   When he experienced a storm in France
    D   While he was on holiday and lightning struck
    E   When he was out walking and he experienced high winds

4 What happened to Hani's parents' car when he was travelling in Italy?
    A   The car broke down.
    B   The windscreen was dented by hailstones.
    C   Golf balls were thrown and hit the car.
    D   The car crashed into a service station.
    E   Hailstones hit the bonnet and the roof.

5 Which of these phrases best describes when Hani's holiday home was hit by lightning?
    A   It occurred in the early hours of the morning and the shutters were ablaze.
    B   It occurred during the day and they avoided a fire.
    C   It occurred at night and forest fires were ablaze.
    D   It occurred at night and the house was ablaze.
    E   It occurred during the day and helicopters were flying overhead.

6 Which of these phrases best describes the weather that Hani has experienced in his home town?

    A   He experienced a flood in a car park.

    B   He experienced a snowstorm at the top of the hill.

    C   He experienced flooding near his home.

    D   He experienced lightning in his garden.

    E   He experienced high winds in his garden.

7 Which of the phrases below best describes Hani's future career choices?

    A   The passage does not say.

    B   He would like to be a storm chaser.

    C   He is undecided at the moment.

    D   He will be studying meteorology.

    E   He will not be studying a science-based degree.

8 Which other members of Hani's family like the weather?

    A   Hani and his cousin

    B   Hani's parents, his cousin and his sister

    C   Hani's parents and his sister

    D   Hani's parents and his brother

    E   Hani's brother and sister

9 What type of word is 'meteorologist'?

    A   noun

    B   adverb

    C   pronoun

    D   adjective

    E   verb

10 Within the context of the passage, what is another word for 'endeavours'?

    A   arguments

    B   tasks

    C   features

    D   energy

    E   efforts

Cloze Wordbank Test 1

TOP TIME MANAGEMENT TIPS

- Quickly read all of the words in the wordbank before you start in order to familiarise yourself with the possible answer options.

- If you know the easier words, complete these questions first. By a process of elimination, you may be able to work out the answer with the words that are still available.

 # INSTRUCTIONS

 You have 6 minutes to complete the following section.
You have 10 questions to complete within the time given.

EXAMPLE

Choose a word to complete the sentence below.

A   jumper
B   big
C   write
D   bone
E   wall
F   worn
G   blue
H   go
I   try
J   jumped

The cat ......①...... over the fence.

The correct answer is J.

Complete the passage below by choosing the correct words from the wordbank.
Write your answers to go in place of each question number 1–10 in the passage.

WORDBANK

A season	**B** comforts	**C** quirky	**D** case	**E** destination
F comparison	**G** round	**H** emergence	**I** trends	**J** caravans

Glamping

The ① .... of the UK as a popular holiday ② .... has given rise to the 'staycation' and other phrases such as 'glamping'. These are popular ways to describe new ③ .... in holidays.

Glamping is camping whilst keeping home ④ .... Many of the holidays are set in beautiful surroundings such as wooded areas or involve a stay in an unusual place such as a yurt, which is a ⑤ .... Mongolian tent. Other places to stay include beach huts, ⑥ .... and eco cabins.

The decision to go glamping in the UK is not driven by low prices, as is the ⑦ .... with traditional camping, which is cheap in ⑧ .... to staying in a hotel. Glamping can be costly and it is often cheaper to buy an 'all-inclusive' holiday, which comprises flights, accommodation, food and drink. However, many families choose glamping because the holiday destinations are ⑨ .... and off the beaten track.

One example of these more unusual destinations is a treehouse, which is sited in a 250-year-old oak tree. In high ⑩ .... prices reach £1000 per night.

Cloze Wordbank Test 2

 You have 5 minutes to complete the following section.
You have 10 questions to complete within the time given.

Complete the passage below by choosing the correct words
from the wordbank.
Write your answers to go in place of each question number
1–10 in the passage.

WORDBANK

A necessity	B commute	C wages	D advised	E unfair
F fares	G campaigning	H machines	I work	J results

Rail tickets

Over 95% of commuters travel to ① _____ I _____ by car. However, there are many people who have to ② _____ B _____ by rail. This is a ③ _____ A _____ which many people in the South-East of England have to factor into their working life.

Annual price rises for season tickets are often much higher than the increase in people's ④ _____ C _____ . There are many action groups which are ⑤ _____ J _____ to reduce the price rises as they feel they are completely ⑥ _____ E _____ . They have campaigned for changes and one of the ⑦ _____ G _____ which has recently been announced is the change to self-service ⑧ _____ H _____ . Commuters must now be informed of any cheaper ⑨ _____ F _____ available and will be ⑩ _____ D _____ to buy this ticket from the ticket office.

Cloze Wordbank Test 3

INSTRUCTIONS

 You have 4 minutes to complete the following section.
You have 10 questions to complete within the time given.

Complete the passage below by choosing the correct words
from the wordbank.
Write your answers to go in place of each question number
1–10 in the passage.

WORDBANK

A street	B revellers	C coordinated	D restricted	E backdrop
F overlooking	G stroke	H popular	I celebrate	J artists

New Year's Eve celebrations

People choose to ① _____ the onset of a new year in many different ways.

On New Year's Eve, thousands of ② _____ travel to London to view the fireworks from key points ③ _____ the River Thames. Numbers were ④ _____ this year as tickets were required. The fireworks and their colourful explosions were seen against a ⑤ _____ of the London skyline.

The fireworks, which commenced on the ⑥ _____ of midnight, were ⑦ _____ in time with music from some of today's most popular ⑧ _____ .

Around the UK, people congregated in the major cities to celebrate. The festivities in Edinburgh are extremely ⑨ _____ for those wishing to attend anything from ⑩ _____ parties to candle-lit concerts.

Cloze Wordbank Test 4

INSTRUCTIONS

You have 4 minutes to complete the following section.
You have 10 questions to complete within the time given.

Complete the passage below by choosing the correct words from the wordbank.
Write your answers to go in place of each question number 1–10 in the passage.

WORDBANK

A fatal	B represents	C rare	D population	E documented
F commonplace	G habitat	H decline	I pine	J Scotland

Red squirrels

The population of red squirrels has, for many years, been in ① _____ , whereas the rise in the population of the grey squirrel is well ② _____ . Grey squirrels were introduced to Britain from America in the nineteenth century.

Few people have seen red squirrels in their garden, although they used to be ③ _____ . Due to conservation projects, red squirrels are now increasingly being spotted in areas where they have not been seen for many years.

In the Highlands of ④ _____ , there are about 90,000 red squirrels. This ⑤ _____ a significant percentage of the total UK squirrel ⑥ _____ . The ⑦ _____ forests in the Highlands are the perfect ⑧ _____ for red squirrels and it is ⑨ _____ to see a grey squirrel.

Red squirrels were under threat for a number of years. There are many reasons why numbers were in decline, one of which was squirrel-pox. Grey squirrels carry the disease without any harm. However, the disease is ⑩ _____ to red squirrels.

Antonyms: Write in the Word Test

TOP TIME MANAGEMENT TIPS

- Some answers may form real words and others are simply letters.
- If you cannot complete a question, write a sensible guess and then move on to the next question.
- Make a note of the questions which you found difficult. Revisit them if you have time remaining at the end.

 INSTRUCTIONS

 You have 6 minutes to complete the following section.
You have 15 questions to complete within the time given.

EXAMPLE

In each question, three letters have been removed from a word. Complete each word.
[I] Complete this word, which is an antonym of **wide**.

nar ....

The correct answer is **narrow** so you should have written the letters 'row'.

In each question, three letters have been removed from a word. Complete each word.

(1) Complete this word, which is an antonym of, or least similar to **closing**.

   o .... ing

(2) Complete this word, which is an antonym of, or least similar to **brave**.

   f .... ful

(3) Complete this word, which is an antonym of, or least similar to **able**.

   in .... able

4 Complete this word, which is an antonym of, or least similar to **rebellious.**

obe .... nt

5 Complete this word, which is an antonym of, or least similar to **irrational.**

reaso .... le

6 Complete this word, which is an antonym of, or least similar to **sociable.**

unfri .... ly

7 Complete this word, which is an antonym of, or least similar to **rigid.**

.... ple

8 Complete this word, which is an antonym of, or least similar to **shapeless.**

sh .... ly

9 Complete this word, which is an antonym of, or least similar to **annoy.**

pl .... e

10 Complete this word, which is an antonym of, or least similar to **mature.**

in .... erienced

11 Complete this word, which is an antonym of, or least similar to **dreary.**

e .... ting

12 Complete this word, which is an antonym of, or least similar to **distant.**

.... se

13 Complete this word, which is an antonym of, or least similar to **passive.**

ac .... e

14 Complete this word, which is an antonym of, or least similar to **boastful.**

hum ....

15 Complete this word, which is an antonym of, or least similar to **asymmetrical.**

bal .... ed

Antonyms: Select the Word Test

TOP TIME MANAGEMENT TIPS

- Read the word shown in the question carefully and then read all of the options.
- Keep reminding yourself whether you are looking for a synonym or an antonym, as it is easy to forget.
- There is also the possibility that an option in the answers could confuse you.

 INSTRUCTIONS

 You have 5 minutes to complete the following section.
You have 15 questions to complete within the time given.

EXAMPLE

Select the word from the grid that is least similar in meaning to the word given:

small

A	B	C	D	E
big	tiny	quick	tight	narrow

The correct answer is A.

In each question, select the word from the grid that is least similar in meaning to the word given.

(1) thrifty

A	B	C	D	E
frugal	arrangement	extravagant	courteous	transpire

(2) preserve

A	B	C	D	E
courage	persevere	squander	keep	jam

(3) liquid

A	B	C	D	E
bottle	consume	water	solid	hydrate

4 ethical

A	B	C	D	E
corrupt	considerate	calm	hospital	operation

5 earnest

A	B	C	D	E
coronary	insincere	kind	submissive	deafening

6 porous

A	B	C	D	E
permeable	pious	leak	unimportant	impermeable

7 solution

A	B	C	D	E
question	inconvenient	unconventional	hospitable	extravagant

8 skinny

A	B	C	D	E
arctic	salty	flatly	argumentative	brawny

9 clear

A	B	C	D	E
transparent	evident	colossal	cloudy	inclement

10 glum

A	B	C	D	E
happy	miserable	glower	reckless	distracted

11 veto

A	B	C	D	E
frustration	hinder	stop	approve	cease

12 scruffy

A	B	C	D	E
messy	scowling	lethargic	customary	tidy

13 dupe

A	B	C	D	E
help	fabricate	separate	serenade	hinder

14 insufficient

A	B	C	D	E
sample	ample	simple	lacking	supple

15 nervous

A	B	C	D	E
fear	occupation	composed	ostentatious	confusion

Synonyms: Write in the Word Test

 You have 7 minutes to complete the following section.
You have 15 questions to complete within the time given.

EXAMPLE

In each question, three letters have been removed from a word. Complete each word.
[1] Complete this word, which is a synonym of **sad**.

dr .... y

The correct answer is **dreary** so you should have written the letters 'ear'.

In each question, three letters have been removed from a word. Complete each word.

(1) Complete this word, which is a synonym of **amusing**.

.... cical

(2) Complete this word, which is a synonym of **organic**.

bio .... ical

(3) Complete this word, which is a synonym of **peaceful**.

t .... quil

(4) Complete this word, which is a synonym of **nurture**.

c .... ish

(5) Complete this word, which is a synonym of **newsworthy**.

.... ical

(6) Complete this word, which is a synonym of **mild**.

tem .... ate

(7) Complete this word, which is a synonym of **eager**.

w .... ing

(8) Complete this word, which is a synonym of **pungent**.

aro ic

9. Complete this word, which is a synonym of **haphazard**.

   er ic

10. Complete this word, which is a synonym of **pacify**.

    soo ....

11. Complete this word, which is a synonym of **jolly**.

    jo l

12. Complete this word, which is a synonym of **create**.

    gene .... e

13. Complete this word, which is a synonym of **image**.

    p .... o

14. Complete this word, which is a synonym of **immune**.

    resist ....

15. Complete this word, which is a synonym of **weakened**.

    debi .... ated

Synonyms: Select the Word Test

INSTRUCTIONS

 You have 6 minutes to complete the following section.
You have 15 questions to complete within the time given.

EXAMPLE

In each question, select the word from the grid that is most similar in meaning to the word given:

loud

A	B	C	D	E
big	noisy	quiet	sad	rough

The correct answer is B.

In each question, select the word from the grid that is most similar in meaning to the word given.

(1) destructive

A	B	C	D	E
graceful	destitute	beneficial	malignant	despicable

(2) rotting

A	B	C	D	E
pure	putrid	pleasant	compact	sustainable

(3) magnificent

A	B	C	D	E
small	vulgar	humble	exorbitant	palatial

(4) pale

A	B	C	D	E
squashed	pallid	flushed	soloist	pessimistic

(5) smiling

A	B	C	D	E
masking	beaming	sincere	wallowing	grimace

6 plaster

A	B	C	D	E
incision	brush	nocturnal	emergency	paste

7 hone

A	B	C	D	E
sharpen	honour	residence	honest	hopeful

8 dismal

A	B	C	D	E
daring	bleak	deplete	dismay	feigned

9 ferry

A	B	C	D	E
inaction	abyss	ferrous	sanctuary	transport

10 shocking

A	B	C	D	E
ghastly	amazing	indistinct	vague	voracious

11 squalor

A	B	C	D	E
destruction	disqualify	destitution	restraint	spotless

12 auspicious

A	B	C	D	E
dangerous	automatic	incorrect	suspicious	promising

13 sullen

A	B	C	D	E
assertive	morose	elated	gregarious	athletic

14 whisk

A	B	C	D	E
whim	observe	aspire	whip	desire

15 grant

A	B	C	D	E
request	demand	bestow	gracious	reject

Shuffled Sentences Test 1

TOP TIME MANAGEMENT TIPS

- Read the words carefully and try to work out the possible theme of the sentence quickly.
- Don't spend too much time on any one question as there may be a difficult question early on!
- Remember that you are searching for a word that does not fit in the sentence.
- Think about words which are often used together in phrases.

 # INSTRUCTIONS

 You have 10 minutes to complete the following section.
You have 15 questions to complete within the time given.

EXAMPLE

The following sentence is shuffled and also contains one unnecessary word. Rearrange the sentence correctly in order to identify the unnecessary word.

threw into through ball bucket the I

A	B	C	D	E
threw	through	ball	the	I

The correct answer is B as 'through' does not fit in the sentence. The sentence should read, 'I threw the ball into the bucket.'

Each of these sentences is shuffled and contains one unnecessary word. Rearrange each sentence correctly in order to identify the unnecessary word from the answer options given.

(1) where to buy available Christmas year this rent or trees were

A	B	C	D	E
buy	to	rent	available	where

(2) and in there was a crisp packet the sky was not a cloud morning winter's it

A	B	C	D	E
morning	packet	crisp	sky	cloud

(3) cleaner that likely need was it soon bin the emptying would

A	B	C	D	E
cleaner	soon	that	need	was

4) to tight required certain swing park spaces was in skill the of a unusually amount

A	B	C	D	E
amount	to	park	swing	tight

5) less party was kept matter for in a the weather the changed the promising minutes of and outlook garden

A	B	C	D	E
matter	kept	weather	changed	party

6) any his tolerated be longer behaviour he not could

A	B	C	D	E
his	longer	behaviour	could	he

7) object and fill the form of the texture sculptress the inspired deeply

A	B	C	D	E
object	inspired	the	fill	and

8) too the cushions area they entrance to seats decided draughty move as was

A	B	C	D	E
cushions	entrance	they	move	seats

9) were the juice number they by drinks a to served supermarket bar customers of delicious attracted the that

A	B	C	D	E
supermarket	they	juice	drinks	bar

10) starting fully exhausted full of the felt exercise woman programme her since and new energy revitalised

A	B	C	D	E
exhausted	revitalised	since	full	starting

11) for for for had they owned hose but house entertaining the some more years wanting space looking were now bigger somewhere

A	B	C	D	E
house	entertaining	hose	wanting	they

12) find hidden antiques of they search bargain frequented prices in fairs gems at

A	B	C	D	E
prices	fairs	frequented	search	find

13) instinct he and than gut happy is with followed the leader more outcome his

A	B	C	D	E
outcome	happy	followed	leader	his

(14) can't affords the fabulous restaurant views hotel's rooftop

A	B	C	D	E
can't	the	restaurant	views	affords

(15) outside both a house out property and is the holiday beautiful inside

A	B	C	D	E
inside	house	both	outside	the

Shuffled Sentences Test 2

INSTRUCTIONS

You have 10 minutes to complete the following section.
You have 15 questions to complete within the time given.

Each of these sentences is shuffled and contains one unnecessary word. Rearrange each sentence correctly in order to identify the unnecessary word.

1. that a I aspects to picture draw number your are there of attention should

A	B	C	D	E
should	number	draw	picture	aspects

2. headlines make the the to days broke after continuing it is repaired first story

A	B	C	D	E
repaired	make	broke	story	continuing

3. Coniston us beautiful to stop our start final Lake the brought breathtakingly

A	B	C	D	E
the	our	brought	start	us

4. and never under competitive pressure used are to they fiercely performing

A	B	C	D	E
never	performing	used	pressure	under

5. be right determined behind was she not to left

A	B	C	D	E
left	behind	right	determined	was

6. been recent location makers has film taste the favoured by dramatic in years

A	B	C	D	E
years	has	taste	recent	location

7. at shift when my 3 pm work into I change stick gear my begins

A	B	C	D	E
shift	begins	gear	stick	change

8. recent supermarkets bean in towards years there discount a in has shift been attitude

A	B	C	D	E
attitude	years	recent	shift	bean

9 due could several be the new possibility discovery now to the discounted

A	B	C	D	E
discovery	could	due	several	possibility

10 of would the new the he space thought now tomato relish

A	B	C	D	E
of	would	he	thought	tomato

11 beginning her front start the slamming door made

A	B	C	D	E
door	slamming	made	beginning	her

12 will her left husband her she won't and to children in everything

A	B	C	D	E
children	she	won't	everything	left

13 latest everyone challenge in was her help willing her to succeed

A	B	C	D	E
was	willing	succeed	everyone	help

14 deep water were in interrupt they was the reluctant waitress to as conversation

A	B	C	D	E
waitress	were	deep	water	reluctant

15 delivered was parcel hesitation her or without speech nerves

A	B	C	D	E
parcel	delivered	without	nerves	was

Non-Verbal Reasoning

Mixed Test 1

 INSTRUCTIONS

 You have 7 minutes to complete the following section.
You have 15 questions to complete within the time given.

EXAMPLES

REFLECTION Example

Select how the following shape or pattern would appear when reflected in the dashed line.

The correct answer is B.

A   B   C   D   E

COMPLETE THE GRID Example

Select the shape that completes the grid.

The correct answer is D.

A   B   C   D   E

CODES Example

Look at the following patterns and identify the missing code for the pattern on the right.

AD   FE   AC   BE

A: BD   **B**: FE   **C**: BC   **D**: FD   **E**: FC

The correct answer is C.

CONNECTION Example

Look at the two shapes on the left immediately below. Find the connection between them and apply it to the third shape.

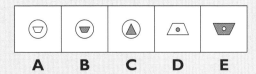

The correct answer is B.

CUBES Example

Look at the cube net below. Select the only cube that could be formed from the net below.

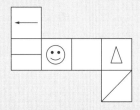

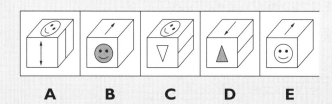

The correct answer is E.

COMPLETE THE SEQUENCE Example

Select the picture from the bottom row that will complete the sequence in place of the ? in the top row.

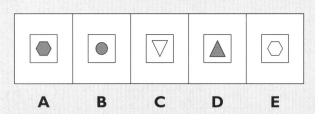

The correct answer is C.

ROTATION Example

Select one of the images below that is a rotation of the image on the left.

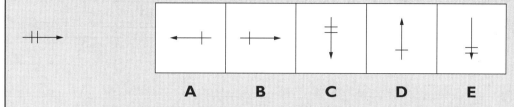

The correct answer is C.

BELONGS TO GROUP Example

The first four patterns form a group. Work out how they are connected and select the option that belongs to the group.

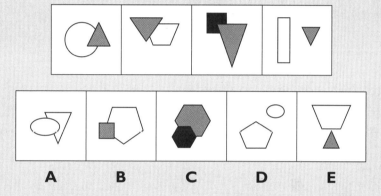

The correct answer is E.

TOP TIME MANAGEMENT TIPS

- Time passes more quickly than you may think. Work out how long you have per question and make sure you don't spend too much time on any one question.

(1) Select the pattern that completes the grid.

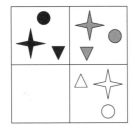

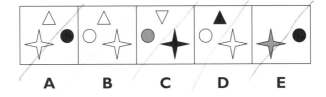

| A | B | C | D | E |

(2) Select the pattern that completes the grid.

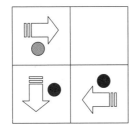

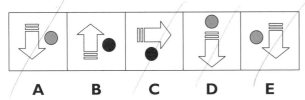

| A | B | C | D | E |

(3) Select the pattern that completes the grid.

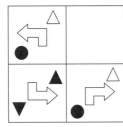

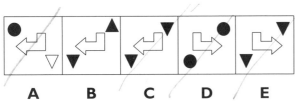

| A | B | C | D | E |

(4) Select the pattern that completes the grid.

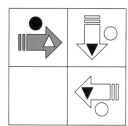

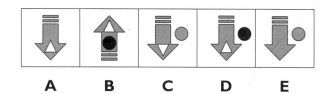

A   **B**   **C**   **D**   **E**

(5) Select the shape that completes the grid.

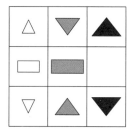

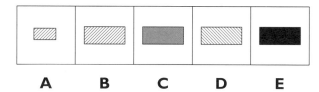

A   **B**   **C**   **D**   **E**

(6) Look at the two shapes on the left immediately below. Find the connection between them and apply it to the third shape.

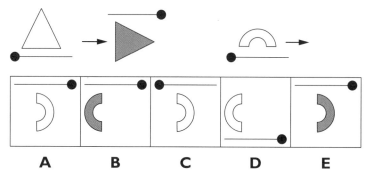

A   **B**   **C**   **D**   **E**

(7) Select how the following shape or pattern would appear when reflected in the dashed line.

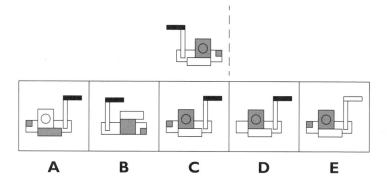

A   **B**   **C**   **D**   **E**

8. Select how the following shape or pattern would appear when reflected in the dashed line.

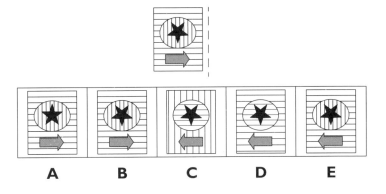

9. Select how the following shape or pattern would appear when reflected in the dashed line.

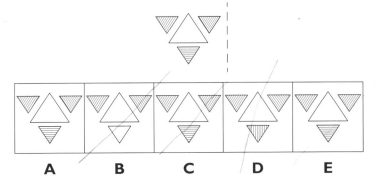

10. The first four patterns form a group. Work out how they are connected and select the option that belongs to the group.

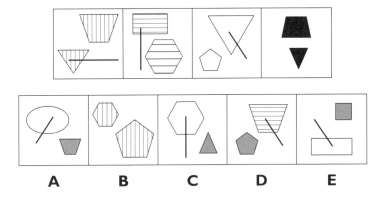

11. The first four patterns form a group. Work out how they are connected and select the option that belongs to the group.

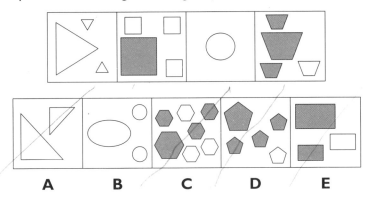

(12) The first four patterns form a group. Work out how they are connected and select the option that belongs to the group.

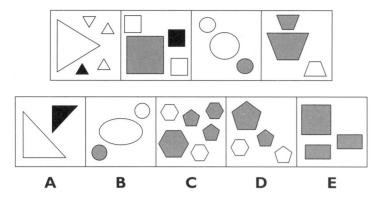

A	B	C	D	E

(13) Select one of the images below that is a rotation of the image on the left.

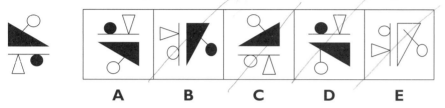

A	B	C	D	E

(14) Select one of the images below that is a rotation of the image on the left.

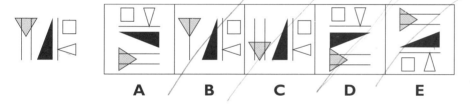

A	B	C	D	E

(15) The first four patterns form a group. Work out how they are connected and select the option that belongs to the group.

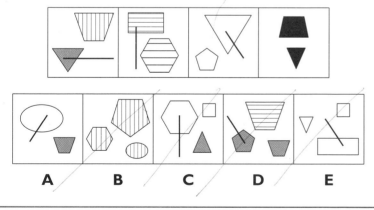

A	B	C	D	E

Mixed Test 2

INSTRUCTIONS

 You have 7 minutes to complete the following section.
You have 15 questions to complete within the time given.

(1) + **(2)** Select the correct pictures from the bottom row in order to finish the incomplete sequence on the top row. One picture should be chosen for Q1 and another picture for Q2.

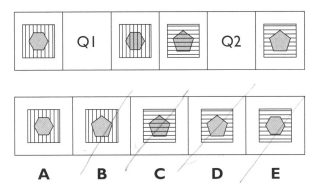

(3) Look at the following patterns and identify the missing code for the pattern on the right.

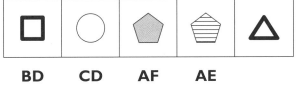

BD   **CD**   **AF**   **AE**

A: AD   **B**: GF   **C**: AE   **D**: GD   **E**: HF

(4) Look at the cube net. Select the only cube that could be formed from the net below.

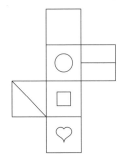

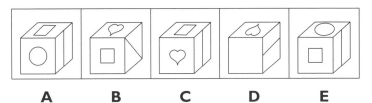

(5) Select the pattern that completes the grid.

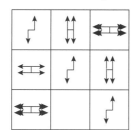

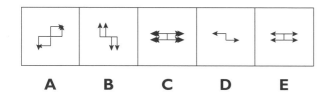

A   B   C   D   E

(6) Look at the cube net. Select the only cube that could be formed from the net below.

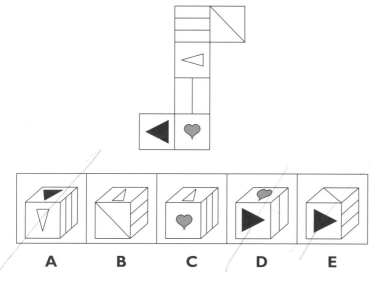

A   B   C   D   E

(7) Select how the following shape or pattern would appear when reflected in the dashed line.

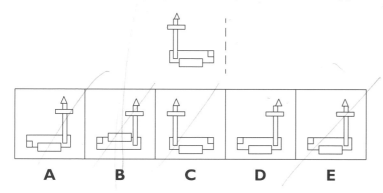

A   B   C   D   E

(8) Select how the following shape or pattern would appear when reflected in the dashed line.

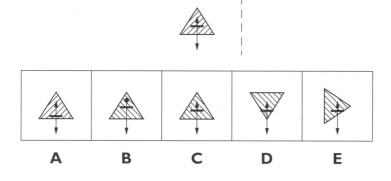

A   B   C   D   E

+10 Select the correct pictures from the bottom row in order to finish the incomplete sequence on the top row. One picture should be chosen for Q9 and another picture for Q10.

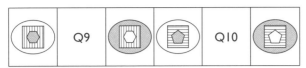

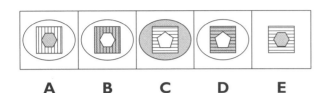

A   B   C   D   E

11 Look at the cube net. Select the only cube that could be formed from the net below.

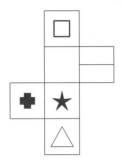

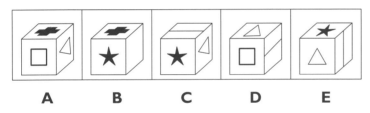

A   B   C   D   E

12 Look at the two shapes on the left immediately below. Find the connection between them and apply it to the third shape.

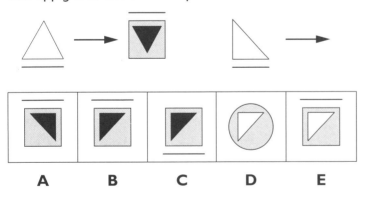

A   B   C   D   E

13 The first four patterns form a group. Work out how they are connected and select the option that belongs to the group.

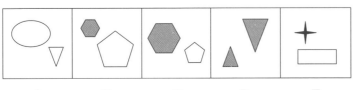

A   B   C   D   E

14 Look at the two shapes on the left immediately below. Find the connection between them and apply it to the third shape.

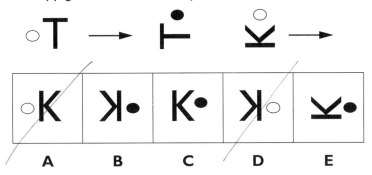

A	B	C	D	E

15 The first four patterns form a group. Work out how they are connected and select the option that belongs to the group.

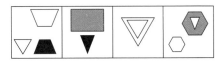

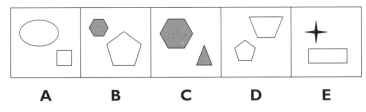

A	B	C	D	E

Mixed Test 3

INSTRUCTIONS

 You have 7 minutes to complete the following section.
You have 15 questions to complete within the time given.

(1) Look at the cube net. Select the only cube from the row below that can be formed from the net.

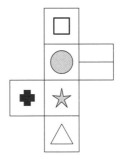

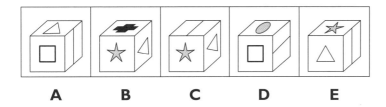

| A | B | C | D | E |

(2) Look at the cube net below. Select the only cube that could be formed from the net below.

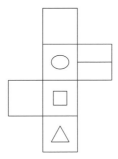

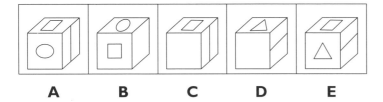

| A | B | C | D | E |

3 Select how the following shape or pattern would appear when reflected in the dashed line.

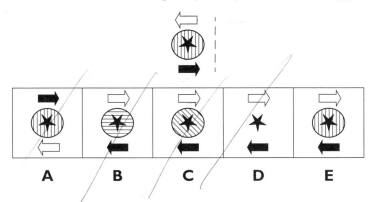

A	B	C	D	E

4 Select the pattern that completes the grid.

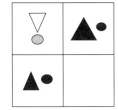

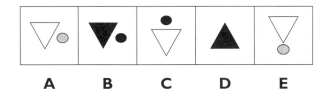

A	B	C	D	E

5 Look at the cube net. Select the only cube that could be formed from the net below.

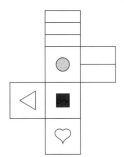

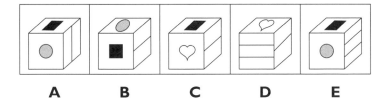

A	B	C	D	E

6 Select the pattern that completes the grid.

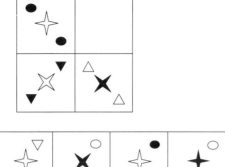

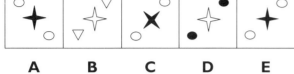

| A | B | C | D | E |

7 Select how the following shape or pattern would appear when reflected in the dashed line.

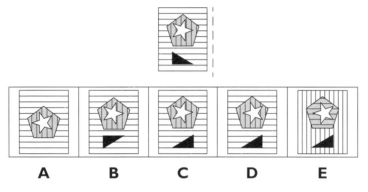

| A | B | C | D | E |

8 Select how the following shape or pattern would appear when reflected in the dashed line.

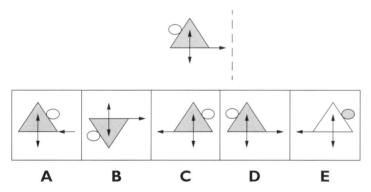

| A | B | C | D | E |

9 Select the pattern that completes the grid.

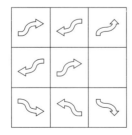

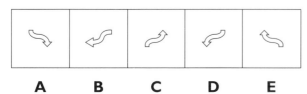

| A | B | C | D | E |

(10) Select the pattern that completes the grid.

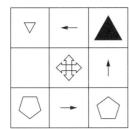

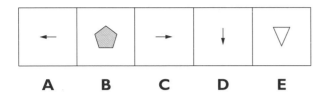

A   **B**   **C**   **D**   **E**

(11) Select the pattern that completes the grid.

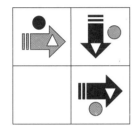

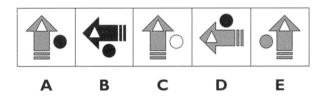

A   **B**   **C**   **D**   **E**

(12) Select one of the images below that is a rotation of the image on the left.

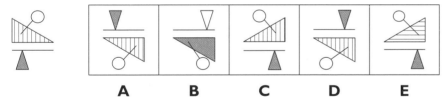

A   **B**   **C**   **D**   **E**

(13) Select the pattern that completes the grid.

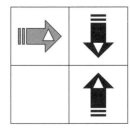

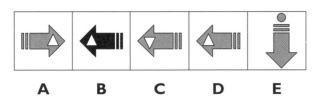

A   **B**   **C**   **D**   **E**

14 The first four patterns form a group. Work out how they are connected and select the option that belongs to the group.

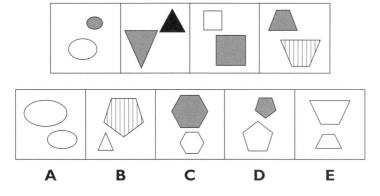

A	B	C	D	E

15 The first four patterns form a group. Work out how they are connected and select the option that belongs to the group.

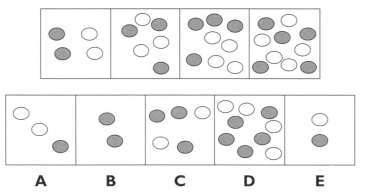

A	B	C	D	E

Mixed Test 4

 You have 7 minutes to complete the following section.
You have 15 questions to complete within the time given.

(1) Look at the two shapes on the left immediately below. Find the connection between them and apply it to the third shape.

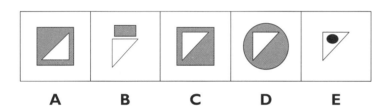

| A | B | C | D | E |

(2) Look at the cube net. Select the only cube that could be formed from the net below.

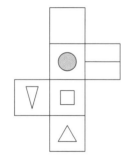

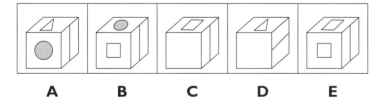

| A | B | C | D | E |

3 Select how the following shape or pattern would appear when reflected in the dashed line.

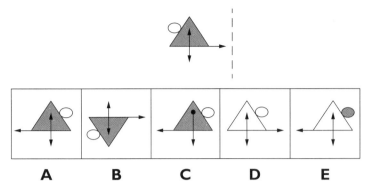

A	B	C	D	E

4 Select one of the images below that is a rotation of the image on the left.

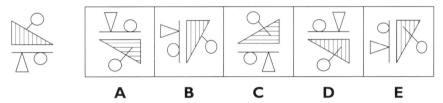

A	B	C	D	E

5 Select the pattern that completes the grid.

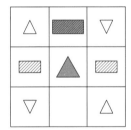

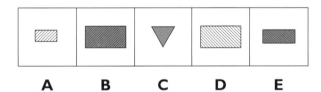

A	B	C	D	E

6 Look at the following patterns and identify the missing code for the pattern on the right.

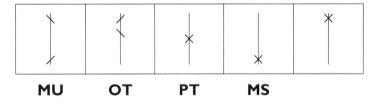

MU   OT   PT   MS

A: MT   **B**: PS   **C**: OS   **D**: PU   **E**: OU

(7) Select how the following shape or pattern would appear when reflected in the dashed line.

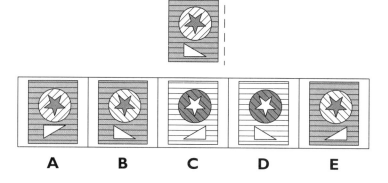

| A | B | C | D | E |

(8) The first four patterns form a group. Work out how they are connected and select the option that belongs to the group.

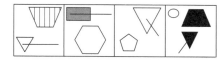

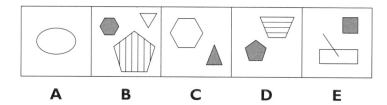

| A | B | C | D | E |

(9) Select one of the images below that is a rotation of the image on the left.

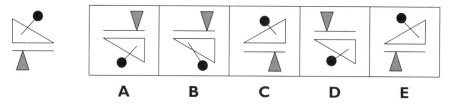

| A | B | C | D | E |

(10) Select how the following shape or pattern would appear when reflected in the dashed line.

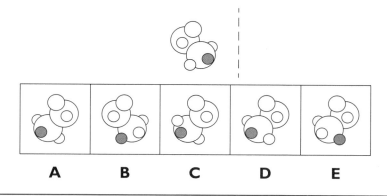

| A | B | C | D | E |

(11) Select how the following shape or pattern would appear when reflected in the dashed line.

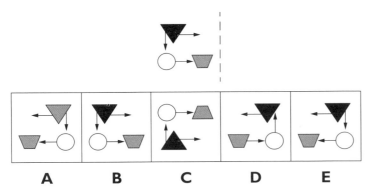

| A | B | C | D | E |

(12) Look at the following patterns and identify the missing code for the pattern on the right.

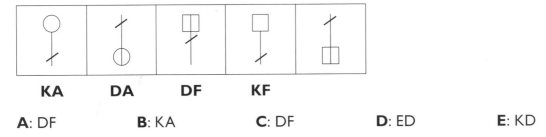

| KA | DA | DF | KF |

A: DF   **B**: KA   **C**: DF   **D**: ED   **E**: KD

(13) Select how the following shape or pattern would appear when reflected in the dashed line.

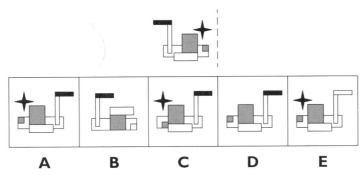

| A | B | C | D | E |

(14) The first four patterns form a group. Work out how they are connected and select the option that belongs to the group.

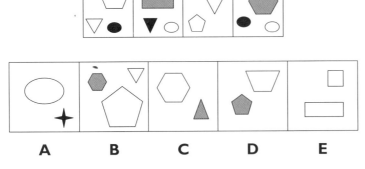

| A | B | C | D | E |

(15) Select one of the images below that is a rotation of the image on the left.

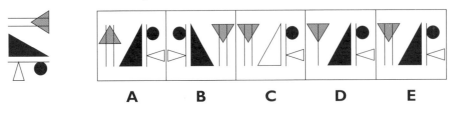

| A | B | C | D | E |

Numeracy & Problem Solving Answers

Mixed Questions Test 1

Q1 17
($51 \div 3$)

Q2 500 ml

Q3 North-West

Q4 43
($774 \div 18$)

Q5 8 hours 40 minutes

Q6 −4
($15.5 - 19.5$)

Q7 3°C

Q8 $410\frac{1}{16}$ cm²
Each side is 20.25 cm (perimeter divided by 4).
The area is $20.25 \times 20.25 = 410\frac{1}{16}$ cm²
0.25 is equivalent to $\frac{1}{4}$. When $\frac{1}{4}$ is
multiplied by $\frac{1}{4}$, this gives $\frac{1}{16}$.

Q9 28
The triangular number sequence is made
from a pattern of dots that form triangles.
By adding a row of dots, containing one
more dot than the previous row, a larger
triangle is made. The number of dots in the
triangle gives the next triangular number
in the sequence. The triangular number
sequence is 1, 3, 5, 10, 15, 21, 28, 36...
Notice that the difference between the
numbers in the sequence increase by 1 each
time (because 1 extra dot is required to
produce the next larger triangle).

Q10 3408

Q11 5020

Q12 £4.80
(Pocket money is £12 as 10% = £1.20).
I spend 40% of £12.

Q13 £42
Original price is 2 × £60 = £120 as I had
saved half of the money. New price is 15%
less than £120 = £102. I now need to save
£102 − £60 = £42.

Mixed Questions Test 2

Q1 $y = 6$
Take one equation from the other to give
$2x = 24$, so $x = 12$. Using this, y must equal 6.

Q2 8
As $\frac{1}{2}$ (or $\frac{3}{6}$) left before 8 pm, then $\frac{1}{2}$ must
leave after 8 pm. $\frac{1}{3}$ (or $\frac{2}{6}$) of the total
remained after midnight. This means $\frac{1}{6}$
leave between 8 pm and midnight, which the
information in the questions tells us is 4. So
24 people were at the party. This means
8 (which is $\frac{1}{3}$ of 24) remained after midnight.

Q3 300 g at 42p
Prices per 100 g (easier for comparison) are
as follows:
15p, 14.2p, 16p, 14p, 16p so the best
value is the cheapest per 100 g which is
300 g as it is 14p per 100 g.

Q4 £240
Convert into twentieths: $\frac{1}{5} \times \frac{4}{4} = \frac{4}{20}$;
$\frac{1}{4} \times \frac{5}{5} = \frac{5}{20}$; first two children get $\frac{4}{20} + \frac{5}{20}$
$= \frac{9}{20}$, so third child gets $\frac{11}{20}$, which is £132.
So $\frac{1}{20}$ is £12 and the amount shared out is
therefore £240.

Q5 4 hours
B is 4 hours ahead of C, or C is 4 hours
behind B. Country A is 8 hours behind
country B, and Country C is 4 hours ahead
of Country A. So Country C is in a time zone
mid-way between Countries A and B.

Q6 10 cm³
Candle burns at 1 cm per hour for 5 hours, so
candle was 5 cm tall to begin with. Therefore
volume initially was $2 \times 5 = 10$ cm³
(Volume of a cylinder is area × height.)

Q7 32
$29 - 17 + 6 + 29 - 15 = 32$ children get
off the bus at the final (fourth) stop.

Q8 Brian is 49 and Fiona is 41
Writing Brian's age as Fiona + 8 years,
then the sum of their ages is
(Fiona + 8) + Fiona = 90
So 2 × Fiona's age, + 8 years, totals
90 years. So this means that 2 × Fiona's
age = 82 years, and therefore Fiona is age
41, and Brian is 41 + 8 = age 49.

Q9 *500*
712 − 212

Q10 *300 miles*
The 15 gallon car tank is $\frac{2}{3}$ full. 10 gallons × 30 miles (the car can travel per gallon) = 300 miles.

Q11 *150 degrees*
(5 × 30) There are 360 degrees on the whole clock, so 30 degrees for each hour. Obtuse angle is greater than 90 degrees and less than 180 degrees.

Q12 *7 years old*
Tom's sister will be 10 on Tom's next birthday. Tom will be 3 years younger, so aged 7.

Q13 *6242 − 1359 = 4883. The top missing number in the units column must have been a 2 initially. Once a '10' is borrowed, this becomes 12. The 4 in the '10's' column will become a 3 (once a '10' is borrowed). A 'hundred' is then borrowed from next column, to give 13 '10's' subtract 5 '10's' makes 8. 12 'hundreds' less one that is borrowed, becomes 11, which when 3 is subtracted gives 8. So the missing hundred is 2. One of the 'thousands' has been borrowed to leave 5 which has 1 'thousand' subtracted from it to give 4.*

Mixed Questions Test 3

Q1 *£190.50*
The 1st and 3rd child receive the same share (12.5% or one eighth).

Q2 *38*
as Terry is 72 this year and Bernice is 77 this year. Bernice will be 78 next year, so Georgie will be 39 next year, which means Georgie is 38 years old now.

Q3 *7 children get on at the second stop*
(23 − 15 + 9 − 6 + ? = 18)

Q4 *1.5 litres at £1.90*
Prices per litre (easier for comparison) are as follows: 135p, 180p, 137.5p, 126.66p, 160p. So best value is 1.5 litres at £1.90 which works out at just under £1.27 per litre.

Q5 *50 miles per gallon*
The tank has 45 litres of fuel inside, which is equivalent to 10 gallons. The car would need to cover 50 miles per gallon in order to be able to travel for 500 miles on this amount of fuel.

Q6 *6*
Joining the 3 pairs of opposite interior angles within a regular hexagon will divide it into 6 equilateral triangles.

Q7 *242*
(927 − 247 − 438)

Q8 *Four people leave the party after 4pm as 36 people leave before 4 pm*
Eight people, which represents 20% of the total guests, leave after 3 pm and before 4 pm. Total guests are 40, and 90% leave before 4pm (90% of 40 = 36).

Q9 *$\frac{5}{8}$ is larger*
Converting the denominator to 24 enables the fractions to be written as $\frac{5}{8} = \frac{15}{24}$ and $\frac{7}{12} = \frac{14}{24}$.

Q10 *42p*
There is one apple more in the first equation, which causes the total cost to rise by 50p (which must be the cost of one apple). Using this fact in either of the equations gives the cost of the pear as 42p.

Q11 *6 hours*
Country B is 6 hours behind Country C, or C is 6 hours ahead of B.

Q12 *300 degrees*
(10 × 30) There are 360 degrees on the whole clock, so 30 degrees for each hour. A reflex angle is greater than 180 degrees.

Q13 *0.1*
(2.105 − 2.005)

Problem Solving Test 1

Q1 *D*
66 months, or 5 years and 6 months from the start of June 2006 to the start of December 2011 (include June and exclude December).

Q2 *G*
38 hours, Monday to Thursday Mira works 8 hours, and 3 hours on Fridays and Saturdays. Total hours 32 + 6 = 38 hours per week.

Q3 *M*
£158,080 (38 hours × £80/h × 52 weeks)

Q4 K

£30,400 per year (38 × 16 × 50). Dentist is paid 5 times as much as Sandra, so Sandra is paid
80 ÷ 5 = £16 per hour. On Monday to Thursday Sandra works 8 hours, and 3 hours on Fridays and Saturdays. Total hours 32 + 6 = 38 hours per week at £16 per hour for 50 weeks.

Q5 B

20%. In the question it says that Sandra is paid one-fifth of what Mira is paid. This is equivalent to 20%.

Q6 C

2 hours 18 minutes. From 07:42 to 08:51 is 1 hour and 9 minutes each way, so 2 hours 18 minutes each day.

Q7 I

£189 per week (9,450 ÷ 50)

Q8 N

£156. Parking is for 6 days per week (Monday to Saturday) at £26 per day, so £26 × 6.

Q9 O

£264. Fuel costs (4 gallons used to travel 80 miles per day) 18 litres is 4 gallons = £18 petrol per day + £26 parking per day. Cost for 6 days in the week that Sandra works is 6 × £44 = £264.

Q10 E

£43.20. Weekly cost is currently 6 × £18 = £108 for fuel. 40% of £108 would be the increase in the fuel cost = 0.4 × 108 = £43.20

Problem Solving Test 2

Q1 N

19 years (2016 − 1997)

Q2 D

18 years old. Jenny is 46 next year, and Jackie 23 next year, so she is 22 now. Four years ago, Jackie was 18 years old.

Q3 G

£567 (£9 × 9 hours per day × 7 days per week)

Q4 H

£120, Sally and Jenny each have six free haircuts with a value of £20 (charge to customers).

Q5 M

£146 (£2 × £73)

Q6 L

£713 (567 from Q3 + 146 from Q5)

Q7 I

£26. Saved £20 for the current haircut, plus 30% off £20 on the next haircut (0.3 × £20 = £6)

Q8 F

3500 (175 × 20)

Q9 K

1926 (321 × 6)

Q10 J

3 haircuts per hour. They each work 8 hours per day (allowing for 1 hour lunch break). Total hours per week (6 days) is 48 each. 96 hours in total (between the two hairdressers). 312 haircuts in 96 hours is just over 3 haircuts per hour. 3 per hour would mean 288 haircuts, whilst 4 per hour would mean 384 haircuts. 3 haircuts per hour is much closer to the 312 average haircuts per week.

Problem Solving Test 3

Q1 D

5.30 pm. Leaving at this time, adding 7 hours' flight duration, then subtracting 5 hours (as New York is 5 hours behind) gives an arrival time of 7.30 pm. The next flight to leave (from the answer options provided) at 6.30 pm, will not arrive until 8.30 pm.

Q2 A

5 minutes and 50 seconds, as 70 ÷ 2 = 35 lots of 10 seconds. 350 seconds is equivalent to 5 minutes and 50 seconds.

Q3 D

The tank is empty. The car has 20 litres of fuel in the tank, out of an available 80 litres. This is equivalent to one quarter of a tank. Using one quarter of a tank means there will be no fuel left after the journey.

Q4 D

44, as 404 ÷ 9 = 44 remainder 8, so only 44 lots of 9 can be subtracted from 404.

Q5 C

Train 2 is the slowest at 3 hours and 12 minutes. Train 1 is 3 hours 7 minutes, train 3 is 2 hours and 48 minutes, and train 4 is 2 hours and 6 minutes.

Q6 C

3 chances in 6, as the faces on a dice are numbered 1 to 6, and 3 out of the 6 faces are numbered more than 3 (4, 5 and 6).

Q7 A

1 as if $4 + 4b = 8$, then $4b = 4$, and so $b = 1$.

Q8 E

$n + 1$, as the value in the sequence is always 1 more than the position of the term in the sequence.

Q9 C

150 cm². Opposite sides of a rectangle are equal, so if $2d - 8 = d + 1$, then by adding 8 to both sides of the equation gives: $2d = d + 9$, which means $d = 9$, as $d + d = d + 9$. Lengths of sides are 15 cm and 10 cm. Area is therefore 15 cm × 10 cm = 150 cm².

Q10 E

−11, as e must be a negative number, so that when it is subtracted from 16, the answer is larger than 16.

Q11 B

3 as adding 10 to both sides gives $4y = 12$, so $y = 3$.

Q12 E

7 as $n^2 + 17 = 66$ (from the question). This means that $n^2 = 66 - 17 = 49$, so $n = 7$ (by taking the square root of both sides).

Q13 B

21. At the start, the dominoes are shared in the ratio 1:2:3 (as Tom has twice as many as Yasmin, and Kerry has three times as many as Yasmin). Start: Yasmin $Y = 8$, Tom $T = 16$, Kerry $K = 24$. By the end $T + 2$, $Y - 2$, and $Y + 3$, $K - 3$ leaving $Y = 8 - 2 + 3 = 9$, $T = 16 + 2 = 18$, and $K = 24 - 3 = 21$.

Q14 E

£5.50 as two adult tickets are equivalent to four child tickets, so effectively, there are the equivalent of nine child tickets (5 + 4). Dividing the total cost by 9 shows that each child ticket costs £5.50.

Q15 A

552 as $46 \times 12 = 552$

Problem Solving Test 4

Q1 240 m²

24 m × 10 m

Q2 32 m²

8 m × 4 m

Q3 48 m³

8 m × 4 m × 1.5 m

Q4 48 tonnes

48 × 1

Q5 24 m²

24 m × 0.5 m × 2

Q6 4%

6 m × 1.5 m = 9 m²

$9 \div 240 = 3 \div 80 = 0.0375$ or 3.75% so 4% to the nearest whole number.

Q7 12 is the denominator

5 m × 4 m = 20m² out of 24 m × 10 m = 240 m²

$\frac{20}{240}$ simplifies to $\frac{1}{12}$.

Q8 2000

(20 × 100). The patio is 20 m². Each m² will fit 10 × 10 = 100 small tiles.

Q9 29 × £65 = £1,885

2000 ÷ 70 is 28 remainder 40 (so 29 boxes will actually be required).

Q10 65%

The non-grass areas add up to $20 + 24 + 32 + 9 = 85$ m². Grass is therefore 155 out of the total area of 240.

$\frac{155}{240} = \frac{31}{48}$. As a percentage this is

$\frac{31}{48} \times 100 = \frac{3100}{48} = \frac{775}{12} = 64\frac{7}{12}$ which, to the nearest whole number, is 65%.

Verbal Reasoning Answers

Comprehension Test 1

Q1 C
challenger

Q2 A
It took over two months to arrive at the Opening Ceremony and it visited many places along the way

Q3 E
The public had mixed feelings about the overall cost of the Olympic Games

Q4 A
A person who has reservations

Q5 B
The local area is now rejuvenated.

Q6 C
People now watch and follow a wider variety of sports.

Q7 C
It was a mixture of lights, music and people.

Q8 B
adjective

Q9 D
A special post box was installed in the town in which they live.

Q10 A
Without parallel

Comprehension Test 2

Q1 B
A significant event in a person's life

Q2 E
At the tennis club

Q3 A
A quiet and amusing personality

Q4 B
The passage does not say

Q5 E
With a delicious breakfast and a handmade card

Q6 D
A set of handcrafted cards for a national attraction

Q7 C
Due to a country show

Q8 E
To be unaware

Q9 B
Upset and nervous

Q10 B
adverb

Comprehension Test 3

Q1 E
Hani likes watching storms and how they affect nature.

Q2 B
threatening

Q3 D
While he was on holiday and lightning struck

Q4 E
Hailstones hit the bonnet and the roof

Q5 C
It occurred at night and forest fires were ablaze.

Q6 C
He experienced flooding near his home.

Q7 C
He is undecided at the moment.

Q8 C
Hani's parents and his sister

Q9 A
noun

Q10 E
efforts

Cloze Wordbank Test 1

Q1 H
emergence

Q2 E
destination

Q3 I
trends

Q4 B
comforts

Q5 G
round

Q6 J
caravans

Q7 D
case
Q8 F
comparison
Q9 C
quirky
Q10 A
season

Cloze Wordbank Test 2

Q1 I
work
Q2 B
commute
Q3 A
necessity
Q4 C
wages
Q5 G
campaigning
Q6 E
unfair
Q7 J
results
Q8 H
machines
Q9 F
fares
Q10 D
advised

Cloze Wordbank Test 3

Q1 I
celebrate
Q2 B
revellers
Q3 F
overlooking
Q4 D
restricted
Q5 E
backdrop
Q6 G
stroke
Q7 C
coordinated
Q8 J
artists

Q9 H
popular
Q10 A
street

Cloze Wordbank Test 4

Q1 H
decline
Q2 E
documented
Q3 F
commonplace
Q4 J
Scotland
Q5 B
represents
Q6 D
population
Q7 I
pine
Q8 G
habitat
Q9 C
rare
Q10 A
fatal

Antonyms: Write in the Word Test

Q1 pen
(opening)
Q2 ear
(fearful)
Q3 cap
(incapable)
Q4 die
(obedient)
Q5 nab
(reasonable)
Q6 end
(unfriendly)
Q7 sup
(supple)
Q8 ape
(shapely)
Q9 eas
(please)
Q10 exp
(inexperienced)

Q11 xci
(exciting)
Q12 clo
(close)
Q13 tiv
(active)
Q14 ble
(humble)
Q15 anc
(balanced)

Q3 ran
(tranquil)
Q4 her
(cherish)
Q5 top
(topical)
Q6 per
(temperate)
Q7 ill
(willing)
Q8 mat
(aromatic)
Q9 rat
(erratic)
Q10 the
(soothe)
Q11 via
(jovial)
Q12 rat
(generate)
Q13 hot
(photo)
Q14 ant
(resistant)
Q15 lit
(debilitated)

Antonyms: Select the Word Test

Q1 C
extravagant
Q2 C
squander
Q3 D
solid
Q4 A
corrupt
Q5 B
insincere
Q6 E
impermeable
Q7 A
question
Q8 E
brawny
Q9 D
cloudy
Q10 A
happy
Q11 D
approve
Q12 E
tidy
Q13 A
help
Q14 B
ample
Q15 C
composed

Synonyms: Write in the Word Test

Q1 far
(farcical)
Q2 log
(biological)

Synonyms: Select the Word Test

Q1 D
malignant
Q2 B
putrid
Q3 E
palatial
Q4 B
pallid
Q5 B
beaming
Q6 E
paste
Q7 A
sharpen
Q8 B
bleak
Q9 E
transport
Q10 A
ghastly

Q11 *C*
destitution

Q12 *E*
promising

Q13 *B*
morose

Q14 *D*
whip

Q15 *C*
bestow

Shuffled Sentences Test 1

Q1 *E where*
Christmas trees were available to rent/buy or buy/rent this year. OR This year Christmas trees were available to buy/rent or rent/buy.

Q2 *B packet*
It was a crisp winter's morning and there was not a cloud in the sky.

Q3 *A cleaner*
It was likely that the bin would need emptying soon.

Q4 *D swing*
A certain amount of skill was required to park in the unusually tight spaces. OR In the unusually tight spaces a certain amount of skill was required to park. OR In the unusually tight spaces to park a certain amount of skill was required.

Q5 *B kept*
The weather changed in a matter of minutes and the outlook for the garden party was less promising.

Q6 *E he*
His behaviour could not be tolerated any longer.

Q7 *D fill*
The form/texture and texture/form of the object inspired the sculptress deeply.

Q8 *A cushions*
They decided to move seats as the entrance area was too draughty. OR As the entrance area was too draughty they decided to move seats.

Q9 *B they*
A number of customers were attracted to the supermarket by the juice bar that served delicious drinks. OR A number of customers were attracted to the juice bar that served delicious drinks by the supermarket. OR A number of customers were attracted to the juice bar by the supermarket that served delicious drinks.

Q10 *A exhausted*
The woman felt full of energy and fully revitalised since starting her new exercise programme. OR Since starting her new exercise programme the woman felt full of energy and fully revitalised.

Q11 *C hose*
They had owned the house for some years but wanting more space for entertaining were now looking for somewhere bigger.

Q12 *E find*
They frequented antiques fairs in search of hidden gems at bargain prices.

Q13 *D leader*
He followed his gut instinct and is more than happy with the outcome.

Q14 *A can't*
The hotel's rooftop restaurant affords fabulous views.

Q15 *D outside*
The holiday house is a beautiful property both inside and out.

Shuffled Sentences Test 2

Q1 *D picture*
There are a number of aspects that I should draw to your attention. OR There are a number of aspects that I should draw your attention to. OR I should draw your attention to a number of aspects that there are.

Q2 *A repaired*
The story is continuing to make the headlines days after it first broke. OR Days after it first broke the story is continuing to make the headlines.

Q3 **D** *start*
Our final stop brought us to the breathtakingly beautiful Lake Coniston. OR Lake Coniston brought us to our breathtakingly beautiful final stop.

Q4 **A** *never*
They are fiercely competitive and used to performing under pressure.

Q5 **C** *right*
She was determined not to be left behind.

Q6 **C** *taste*
The dramatic location has been favoured by film makers in recent years. OR In recent years the dramatic location has been favoured by film makers.

Q7 **D** *stick*
I change into my work gear when my shift begins at 3 pm. OR I change into my work gear at 3 pm when my shift begins. OR When my shift begins at 3 pm I change into my work gear.

Q8 **E** *bean*
There has been a shift in attitude towards discount supermarkets in recent years. OR In recent years there has been a shift in attitude towards discount supermarkets.

Q9 **D** *several*
The possibility could now be discounted due to the new discovery. OR Due to the new discovery the possibility could now be discounted.

Q10 **E** *tomato*
He would now relish the thought of the new space. OR He would relish the thought of the new space now.

Q11 **D** *beginning*
The slamming front door made her start. OR The front door slamming made her start. OR Slamming the front door made her start.

Q12 **C** *won't*
She left everything to her husband/children and children/husband in her will. OR In her will she left everything to her husband/children and children/husband. OR She left everything in her will to her husband/children and children/husband.

Q13 **E** *help*
Everyone was willing her to succeed in her latest challenge.

Q14 **D** *water*
The waitress was reluctant to interrupt as they were deep in conversation. OR They were reluctant to interrupt as the waitress was deep in conversation. OR As they were deep in conversation the waitress was reluctant to interrupt. OR As the waitress was deep in conversation they were reluctant to interrupt.

Q15 **A** *parcel*
Her speech was delivered without hesitation/nerves or nerves/hesitation.

Non-Verbal Reasoning Answers

Mixed Test 1

Q1 B

In each square: all shapes must be the same colour (B is the only possible option).

Q2 A

From bottom row to top row: arrow rotates a quarter turn anti-clockwise; circle turns grey and moves to other side of arrow.

Q3 B

In diagonally opposite squares: arrows are reflected in vertical mirror line; smaller shapes do not change.

Q4 D

From top row to bottom row: arrow and black dot (together) turn a quarter-turn clockwise; triangle remains facing same direction.

Q5 E

Shapes constant in rows; background colour constant in columns.

Q6 E

White shape turns grey and rotates a quarter-turn clockwise; black line with black dot switches from top to bottom and from left to right.

Q7 C

In mirror image: ensure correct position of small grey square and black bar.

Q8 E

In mirror image: ensure arrow remains facing the line of symmetry and stripes are correct.

Q9 A

In mirror image: ensure correct diagonal stripes on top triangles (mirror image is identical to original shape).

Q10 B

In each image: the shading/pattern on all shapes is the same.

Q11 D

In each image: all shapes are the same; total number of shapes matches the number of sides of the featured shape.

Q12 A

In each image: all shapes are the same, just different sizes (shading is irrelevant).

Q13 A

A shows the original image rotated a half-turn (other options can be eliminated by looking at shading and the relationships between images).

Q14 A

A shows the original image rotated a quarter-turn anti-clockwise (other options can be eliminated by looking at shading and the relationships between images).

Q15 A

In each image: two shapes (shading and additional lines are irrelevant).

Mixed Test 2

Q1 D

Left to right: stripes alternate from vertical to horizontal; shape alternates from hexagon to pentagon; looking at pentagons only: shapes alternate from foreground to background in relation to stripes.

Q2 A

Left to right: stripes alternate from vertical to horizontal; shape alternates from hexagon to pentagon; looking at hexagons only: shapes alternate from foreground to background in relation to stripes.

Q3 D

GD: first letter relates to type of shape; second letter relates to colour/shading of shape.

Q4 E

E shows net folded without any rotation (all other nets can be eliminated by looking at the relationships between shapes/patterns on adjoining faces).

Q5 E

Top left to bottom right: shapes are identical on diagonal lines.

Q6 B

B shows net folded and rotated through a quarter-turn clockwise (all other nets can be eliminated by looking at the relationships between shapes/patterns on adjoining faces).

Q7 E

In mirror image: ensure correct position of triangle (slightly towards symmetry line).

Q8 C

In mirror image: ensure diagonal stripes are in opposite direction and arrow ends are correct.

Q9 C

Left to right: small shape alternates from hexagon to pentagon; looking at pentagons only: shapes alternate from white to grey; stripes are always horizontal; colour of large oval is always different from pentagon.

Q10 A

Left to right: small shape alternates from hexagon to pentagon; looking at hexagons only: shapes alternate from grey to white; stripes are always vertical; colour of large oval is always different from hexagon.

Q11 C

C shows net folded and rotated through a quarter-turn anti-clockwise (all other nets can be eliminated by looking at the relationships between shapes/patterns on adjoining faces).

Q12 B

Line switches from bottom to top; triangle inverts, becomes black and sits inside a grey square.

Q13 D

In each image: two shapes; the same shape but different sizes (position and shading is irrelevant).

Q14 B

Letter rotates a quarter-turn anti-clockwise; circle changes to black and moves to other side of letter.

Q15 C

In each image: at least one triangle.

Mixed Test 3

Q1 A

A shows net folded without any rotation and triangle wrapped around to be on top of square (all other nets can be eliminated by looking at the relationships between shapes/ patterns on adjoining faces).

Q2 E

E shows net folded without any rotation (all other nets can be eliminated by looking at the relationships between shapes/patterns on adjoining faces).

Q3 E

In mirror image: ensure correct position and direction of arrows and correct stripe pattern.

Q4 E

In diagonally opposite squares: triangle is enlarged; no change to circle.

Q5 C

C shows net folded without any rotation (all other nets can be eliminated by looking at the relationships between shapes/patterns on adjoining faces).

Q6 E

From bottom row to top: central star rotates 45 degrees anti-clockwise; triangles become circles and swap corners; shading changes from black to white.

Q7 D

In mirror image: ensure top of star points to the left.

Q8 C

In mirror image: ensure correct position of arrows, circle and triangle.

Q9 D

Middle row: arrow from top row rotated a half-turn; images on the bottom row are a reflection (in a vertical line) of the images on the middle row.

Q10 D

Looking at arrows only: arrows point around grid in anti-clockwise direction.

Q11 A

From right to left: arrows change from black to grey and rotate a quarter turn anti-clockwise; triangle inverts; circle turns black.

Q12 D

D shows the original shape rotated a half-turn (other options can be eliminated by looking at shading and the relationships between shapes).

Q13 C

From right to left: arrow rotates quarter turn anti-clockwise and turns grey; triangle inverts.

Q14 D

In each image: two shapes; the same shape but different sizes and different shading; the smaller shape must be at the top.

Q15 E

In each image: an equal number of white and grey ovals.

Mixed Test 4

Q1 C

Outer shape inverts, becomes smaller and is enclosed within a large grey square; inner shape disappears.

Q2 B

B shows net folded without any rotation (all other nets can be eliminated by looking at the relationships between shapes/patterns on adjoining faces).

Q3 A

In mirror image: ensure there is an arrowhead at both ends of the vertical line.

Q4 D

D shows the original image rotated a half-turn clockwise (other options can be eliminated by looking at shading and the relationships between shapes).

Q5 E

Bottom row: shapes are a reflection of the top row in a horizontal mirror line.

Q6 E

OU: first letter relates to position of diagonal line that rises from left to right; second letter relates to position of diagonal line that falls from left to right.

Q7 E

In mirror image: ensure white triangle points in opposite direction to original image and direction of diagonal stripes in circle is reversed.

Q8 E

In each image: a black line overlapping a shape.

Q9 A

A shows the original shape rotated a half-turn (other options can be eliminated by looking at shading and the relationships between shapes).

Q10 D

In mirror image: look at lower half of image and ensure small grey and white circles are reflected correctly.

Q11 E

In mirror image: ensure all arrows are reflected correctly.

Q12 C

DF: first letter relates to whether the shape is in front or behind the vertical line; second letter relates to the type of shape.

Q13 A

In mirror image: ensure position of small grey square is correct.

Q14 E

In each image: the sum of the number of sides of all of the shapes is 8.

Q15 E

E shows the original shape rotated a quarter-turn anti-clockwise (other options can be eliminated by looking at shading and the relationships between shapes).

Test Type	Pages	Date of First attempt	Score	Date of second attempt	Score	Date of third attempt	Score
Numeracy and Problem Solving							
Mixed Questions Test 1	4–5						
Mixed Questions Test 2	6–7						
Mixed Questions Test 3	8–9						
Problem Solving Test 1	10–11						
Problem Solving Test 2	12–13						
Problem Solving Test 3	14–16						
Problem Solving Test 4	17						
Verbal Reasoning							
Comprehension Test 1	18–21						
Comprehension Test 2	22–24						
Comprehension Test 3	25–28						
Cloze Wordbank Test 1	29–30						
Cloze Wordbank Test 2	31						
Cloze Wordbank Test 3	32						
Cloze Wordbank Test 4	33						
Antonyms: Write in the Word Test	34–35						
Antonyms: Select the Word Test	36–37						
Synonyms: Write in the Word Test	38–39						
Synonyms: Select the Word Test	40–41						
Shuffled Sentences Test 1	42–44						
Shuffled Sentences Test 2	45–46						
Non-Verbal Reasoning							
Mixed Test 1	47–53						
Mixed Test 2	54–57						
Mixed Test 3	58–62						
Mixed Test 4	63–66						

Notes